P9-BZM-642

THE RISK-DRIVEN
BUSINESS MODEL

THE RISK-DRIVEN BUSINESS MODEL

FOUR QUESTIONS THAT WILL DEFINE YOUR COMPANY

KARAN GIROTRA AND SERGUEI NETESSINE

Harvard Business Review Press
Boston, Massachusetts

Library of Congress Cataloging-in-Publication Data

Girotra, Karan.
 The risk-driven business model : four questions that will define your company / Karan Girotra, Serguei Netessine.
  pages cm
 ISBN 978-1-4221-9153-8 (hardback)
1. Strategic planning. 2. Business planning. 3. Organizational change.
I. Netessine, Serguei. II. Title.
 HD30.28.G567 2014
 658.4'012—dc23

2013050674

The paper used in this publication meets the requirements of the American National Standard for Permanence of Paper for Publications and Documents in Libraries and Archives Z39.48-1992.

ISBN: 9781422191538
eISBN: 9781422191545

CONTENTS

THE RISK-DRIVEN
BUSINESS MODEL

CHAPTER 1

Archimedes' Lever

The ancient Greek mathematician Archimedes is known, among other things, for his elegant explanation of the physics of levers—applying a relatively lesser force to produce an outsized change. There are many different versions of his most famous quote, but we like this one best: "Give me a lever long enough, and a fulcrum strong enough on which to place it, and I will move the world." Though Archimedes was indulging in slight hyperbole, he expressed an essential truth: by applying the right tools in the right ways, laborers were able to move weights vastly greater than they could unaided.

In the spirit of Archimedes, our book is devoted to moving the world. By making seemingly small modifications to your business models *in a programmatic way*, you will find that you can create significant—even game-changing—competitive differences.

At its heart, this book is about how the key choices you make in designing your business models will either increase or reduce two characteristic types of risk—*information risk* and *incentive-alignment risk*. Defined simply, information risk is a feature of a business model that requires you to *make decisions without sufficient information*. Incentive-alignment risk arises when *the incentives imposed by a business model lead to actions that clash with the broader interests of a value chain*.

Both of these types of risk, which we will explore in detail throughout the book, can create business-model inefficiencies that powerfully affect performance.[1] Becoming mindful of these risks' potentially damaging effects will help you design business models that minimize their impact and therefore perform at the highest level. To this end, this book will empower aspiring entrepreneurs and experienced managers alike with an actionable approach for designing better business models—the four W's approach. By changing *what* decisions are made in the business model, *when* they are made, *who* makes them, and *why* they are made, you will be able to come up with business models that better manage information and incentive risks and, as a result, outperform existing business models, disrupt established ways of doing business, and lead to a sustainable competitive advantage. By the end of this book, you will learn how:

- Diapers.com, MinuteClinic, Narayana Hrudayalaya Hospital, Volkswagen, LAN Airlines, and Tankers International innovated their business models by changing *what* decisions comprise their business models.

- Benetton, American Airlines, Caesars, InnoCentive, Hypios, LiveOps, MyFab, and Kickstarter innovated their business models by changing *when* decisions are made.

- Walmart, Zara, Google, Objective Logistics, Amazon.com, Netafim, and many energy-efficiency service companies innovated their business models by changing *who* makes the decisions.

- The US Department of Defense, Li & Fung, Quad/Graphics, Blockbuster, and TerraPass innovated their business models by changing *why* decisions are made.

What managers perhaps find surprising and poorly understand is that business model innovation (BMI) entails relatively lower degrees of difficulty and uncertainty than traditional forms of product innovation. Producing significant benefits demands neither a new breakthrough technology nor the creation of a brand-new market; a BMI opportunity delivers *existing* products based on *existing* technologies to *existing* markets. This reduces overall uncertainty and makes outcomes more predictable and measurable. Likewise, the hard costs for innovating business models are low, typically requiring little more investment than management time, attention, and analysis. Anyone with business training can play; you don't need to be an engineer or have a black belt in algorithms.

Businesses large and small are candidates, as are firms in industries in which other types of innovation often fail, such as service or commodity businesses. Those shopping for inspiration can forage in unexpected places, since many business model innovations can be freely transferred across diverse industries and geographies. And because BMIs often involve changes that are invisible to other companies, BMIs can bring advantages that are harder to copy and easier to sustain for a longer time. (Even when managers do see a new business model, they often fail to recognize its superiority. For example, for decades, skeptics in the US auto industry dismissed the much-studied Toyota Production System, which resulted in deep competitive disadvantages.)

Innovating business models in established companies can be far more difficult than in new ones; established firms are often the captives of their industries' entrenched ways of doing things, whereas new businesses tend to differentiate by breaking the mold of old practices. One of the objectives of BMI is therefore to question many of the key decisions and assumptions around which firms design business models, and to identify points of leverage where they can unlock new value and can eliminate, reduce, or better tolerate sources of information risk and incentive-alignment risk.

Some business model innovations amount to a clever new twist on an established model. As such, they require little more than the capacity to envision an old business in a new way. Even a simple change can have dramatic effects. For example, Zipcar upended the typical arrangements of the car-rental industry by creating a car-sharing membership model for people in large urban centers (or at universities) who don't own cars but need one occasionally, typically for local use or maybe a weekend outing. The traditional rental-car model, which trades in increments of one or more days, faces a problem of off-peak underutilization of large fleets of expensive cars. But Zipcar customers (known as Zipsters) can rent cars by the hour. While traditional rental cars often sit unrented or else are unused for much of the time they are rented, Zipcars tend to be booked for active use by multiple members during the course of a day, with members paying only for the time they need. Members who have a regular recurring need can prepay $50 monthly, which buys about eight hours of use.

What the founders of Zipcar did—simply by changing the increment of *what* was being offered for sale—was to attract a set of customers that had been shut out of the traditional car-rental model. They aligned what the firm wants to sell with what the customer wants to buy. Suddenly, purchasing an hour or two of access to a car became much easier and more appealing to the many city dwellers who didn't own one. Other key elements of the Zipcar experience followed:

- Using a Zipcar is unlike the usual experience of renting a car. After initially signing up, a member does not need to fill out new paperwork for each use of a car.

- There's no trip to a central rental-car office. Members reserve online and receive directions to the location of the nearest Zipcar.

- When they're done using the car, members return it to the reserved parking spot where they picked it up.

Zipcar's five-word marketing slogan—"wheels when you need them"—sums up the ease, informality, and utility of the offering. In early 2013, rental-car heavyweight Avis bought Zipcar for $500 million, promising to leverage its infrastructure, experience, and scale to take Zipcar to the next level of profitability.[2] No matter how the deal turns out (one long-standing Zipster told the *New York Times*, "Please tell [Avis] not to screw it up"), the car-sharing model is beginning to capture the imaginations of even old-line rental industry players.

There is great competitive urgency for established businesses to embrace BMI, because doing so may provide a potent hedge against losing ground to disruptive upstarts, like Zipcar, that seem to come out of nowhere. Common wisdom indicates that it's better to disrupt yourself than to be disrupted by somebody else. Still, most businesses aren't very good at self-disruption. Business model innovation is a powerful tool for changing that track record.

Growing BMI into a Discipline

BMI isn't new. As some of our examples will demonstrate, companies have practiced BMI sporadically in the past, but typically not in a systematic way and certainly not with an orderly, well-defined, and repeatable process. Indeed, many instances of BMI are one-off gambits arising out of dire business straits. Even innovators often fail to recognize a wider opportunity lurking beyond their expedient response to a business crisis.

Take the case of Blockbuster, the video-rental pioneer that has now fallen on hard times. (Some of the examples we use are of BMIs executed by once-stellar companies whose glory has since faded or by relative newcomers that haven't made it yet. Nothing in business is guaranteed, but there is still plenty to learn both from bygone successes and from interesting experiments whose fate remains uncertain.)

In the mid-1990s, Blockbuster was paying $65 for every VHS tape it ordered from movie producers. At $65, Blockbuster had to rent out each tape more than twenty times at $3 per rental to break even. With these economics, stocking enough tapes in each of its stores to satisfy the high demand for newly released popular films was impossible. Instead, Blockbuster deliberately limited availability in the first weeks of a new release. Hot titles were in short supply from the moment they came out, and customers were forced to wait until demand died down. Sumner Redstone, CEO of Blockbuster's corporate parent, Viacom, diagnosed a business model problem: "It was simply too expensive to stock enough copies of every movie the customers requested . . . [Thirty percent] of people who walked into Blockbuster stores were walking out with nothing. The Blockbuster management had a phrase for it: 'managed dissatisfaction.'"[3]

It was more like industry-engineered dissatisfaction. The studios enjoyed the high margins, thanks to the $65 per tape Blockbuster paid them and the negligible marginal cost of producing a tape. But this price also limited the units of these tapes sold. On Blockbuster's side, new releases accounted for 80 percent of Blockbuster's revenues, yet it couldn't effectively exploit those first weeks of highest demand. Thus, it struggled with economics that both irritated customers through chronic stock-outs and depressed revenue during the peak new-release rental window. The video-rental industry value chain left a lot of money on the table. Blockbuster was routinely turning away customers who were willing to rent a tape for a price higher than the cost of manufacturing it.

Seeking a way out of this bind, Blockbuster proposed a change to its business model—one that altered *why* the tape-stocking decision was made the way it was. In the new model, studios would charge the far more agreeable (and still profitable) price of $3 per tape. In exchange for that dramatic reduction, Blockbuster offered to split rental revenues fifty-fifty with the studios. That would enable it to order many more copies of each new title since this price required only a few rentals—rather than twenty or more—to break even. Blockbuster's video availability and rental revenues soared. Studios gained both on the volume of tapes sold and from their half of the much-enhanced rental revenues. Customers were happier because they made fewer fruitless trips down Blockbuster's aisles. Changing the incentives that drove the tape-stocking decision greatly expanded the value chain's profits. The studios' and Blockbuster's shares of the bigger overall pie were both larger than their original profits.[4] The studios, Blockbuster, and the customers all came out ahead.

By acting to realign the incentives in its value chain to everyone's benefit, Blockbuster lived to fight another day. Yet the company seemed not to have fully grasped the long-term lessons of its near-term salvation. What might have happened if Blockbuster had developed the practice of business model innovation to a well-honed discipline? Might it have avoided some of its later difficulties, like losing market share to Netflix and other players and ultimately going bankrupt? That question is hard to answer, but we believe that Blockbuster could have identified other promising BMI opportunities and would have profited from exploiting them.

The aim of this book is to present BMI in a new light—as an activity worthy of becoming a fully developed enterprise competency. To that end, we offer a framework and guidelines—all illustrated with examples—that will help you take BMI to the level of a reliable, repeatable, improvable, and predictable discipline. But you can't get there without first understanding where you are right now. So, the real starting point of our framework is an audit of your existing business models (or those under development), with the goal of identifying flaws in their design that may be inhibiting opportunities, causing value to be lost.

We believe that by the time you've finished reading this book, you will have ideas, tools, and techniques that will enable you to move the world.

What Counts as Innovation?

Blockbuster is far from alone in having failed to fully embrace on business model innovation. When the company conceived its revenue-sharing idea in 1997, the term BMI didn't even exist and the idea of it was part of "strategy." Even now, BMI remains an emergent category of innovation. Most managers are accustomed to thinking about innovation in the Steve Jobsian context of clever, elegantly designed, technological objects. But it's important to remember that among Jobs's greatest innovations was the singular business model of the iTunes Store. No longer did consumers need to purchase whole albums to get the two or three best songs they really wanted. The Apple model allowed every music lover to curate his or her own unique collection for less than a dollar a tune. Thomas Edison invented the lightbulb, but he also invented the business model whereby electric power was generated, transmitted, metered, and purchased so that the bulb could be lit. Otherwise, there would have been no market for lightbulbs. Jobs and Apple invented the iPod, but they also invented a customer-empowering content-distribution model as complete in its conception as was Edison's grid.

Jobs's BMI made the iPod vastly more valuable to customers. A BMI is thus not the tangible product per se, but all of the dynamic mechanisms that surround the product, both before and after sale, which together make it more attractive, useful, and easier to say yes to. BMI therefore encompasses all of the decisively different ways in which a tangible product is marketed, delivered to customers, or enhanced with services.

While most businesses are well accustomed to following established processes for funding and developing products—R&D budgets in some industries are as high as 20 percent of sales—they are far less focused or programmatic when it comes to BMI. To be sure, the work of business model innovation is not very capital intensive, which is certainly part of its appeal. But, ironically, that has helped to keep it an ad hoc, seminomadic endeavor carved out of strategy, marketing, logistics, research, business development, or divisional operating budgets. Being nomadic, BMI has not yet developed consistent standards and recognized best practices or, in many cases, persisted in enterprises beyond the life span of particular projects or initiatives. An especially pernicious effect of BMI's low profile is that when newly innovated tangible products have trouble getting traction in the marketplace, their champions look first for a technological answer, often ignoring evidence that the problem may rest within the business model itself. In many such cases, BMI never emerges as the source of potential solutions. Consequently, products that might have succeeded are judged as failures because they lacked the right model to support them, either before or after their launch.

We hope, therefore, to give business model innovation a solid push toward becoming a formalized discipline. By developing a framework for practicing BMI, we believe we can help you make a case for its ongoing value so that your companies will make a place for it in their portfolio of innovation strategies.

In the next sections of this chapter, we offer a basic grounding in our framework. Succeeding chapters will describe how the framework's elements play out in specific cases. We draw on dozens of real-world BMIs to show how, by applying our approach, you can design new business models and defang their associated risks and inefficiencies.

The Key Decisions and Risks in Every Business Model

The first key step to understanding how BMI opportunities can be developed is to realize that every business model, without exception, imposes a number of key decisions on the business. We call these key decisions and the context in which they are made the *decision pattern.*

Take, for example, the fashion apparel industry. An apparel manufacturer needs to decide what assortment of garments to offer, in what designs and at what quality; where to source their manufacture; what quantities of which kinds of garments to make and how to get them to market efficiently; and what prices to charge, both at product launch and later in the selling season as demand declines. Taken together, the key components of the decision pattern influence the actions of the apparel manufacturer itself, and the behavior of its customers and its partners.

Our study of key decisions has led us to conclude that the existing pattern of decisions often leads to inefficiencies (or risks) in the business model. For instance, the apparel manufacturer might face the demand risk because it must take a bet on a particular apparel style before knowing whether consumers will love it or hate it (*information risk*). Alternatively, the marketing and the operations departments of the retailer might suffer from the lack of coordination (*alignment risk*) because the former is traditionally evaluated based on maximizing sales, while the latter is traditionally evaluated based on minimizing costs. The path to reinventing the business model then lies in changing how decisions are made so decisions are the levers for inventing (and reinventing) new business models. Our framework identifies four basic types of interventions an innovator might choose to make to a decision pattern: changing *what* decisions the business model involves; *when* a decision is made; *who* should make the decision; and *why* the decision maker makes the decision the way he does.

You can modify these four W's of a business model's decision pattern to improve its performance by addressing the damaging inefficiencies caused by information risk or incentive-alignment risk—and sometimes both. Next is a fuller description of how these four levers operate.

The *What*

Every key business model decision is predicated on an organization's earliest foundational choices. In other words, the firm has chosen to offer a particular set of products or services in a particular way, and those prior choices drive what substantive matters the business model addresses. For example, in deciding what to sell, a 2005 start-up called Quidsi (better known as Diapers.com) focused narrowly on being an internet retailer of diapers and related products, whereas Amazon.com (which eventually acquired Quidsi) chose to focus broadly, branching out from books to sell virtually anything, including diapers.

The choice of what you want your business model's decisions to accomplish can increase or decrease its efficiency. There are a number of ways you might want to change the business model's underlying *what*. For example, if you were a wireless telecom provider burdened by slow collections and high bad debt, you might decide to focus on the prepaid market segment. Or if you were an apparel company seeking to minimize the risks of trying to anticipate volatile consumer demand, you might decide to produce hosiery instead of fashionable dresses. It would all depend on your objectives. Some choices are simply better than others at maximizing the value created within an economic system.

The previous choices on which you founded your business frequently become the fixed starting point for everything you do. That invariably places constraints on the directions in which you might be willing or able to take your business model. Blockbuster chose to have neighborhood retail stores to which customers would come to rent VHS movies, and the key decisions of its business model necessarily reflected that core identity. When Netflix developed a model that challenged Blockbuster's identity, it caught the market leader napping. Blockbuster was too invested in its brick-and-mortar model to respond quickly enough. Assuming you're not an entrepreneurial start-up, therefore, it is only possible to change the *what* of an established business model by revisiting and challenging prior assumptions.

The *When*

The architecture of the business model imposes timing for every decision, or when decisions are made. You must make many of the decisions imposed by your business model before you have enough information to make them with confidence. Thus, the timing of decisions plays a key role in the information risk they bring to your business model. For example, businesses often must decide far in advance to do such risky things as build new factories or invest in long-horizon research. First-movers in adopting a new technology are willing to take on far greater risk because they stand to reap the highest rewards if their moves bear fruit. Fast-followers can profit from the lessons of first-movers' missteps by building a better, lower-risk model. In general, the costlier it is to reverse the consequences of a decision, the more intensely its timing will affect the level of risk. Further, the time between when you make a decision and when you have sufficient information to make the decision defines its information risk.

If you can modify your business model by changing when decisions are made, you will have reduced information risk and the inefficiencies it creates. Online furniture maker MyFab created an innovation to reduce information risk by incentivizing customers to vote for their favorite proposed designs from among a large catalog of possibilities. MyFab would manufacture only the designs that earned the most customer votes. Rather than guess what demand might be at an earlier point in the business process, this type of model allows the *when* of deciding on the assortment and style of goods to wait until clear evidence of customer preferences is available.

The *Who*

A particular person (or persons)—an employee, a government regulator, a committee, or other organizational structure—makes every decision that a business model induces. Ideally, the decision maker relies on the best available information so as to maximize the value created by the decision. Obviously, the choice of decision maker affects both information risk (since different decision makers are informed to varying degrees) and incentive-alignment risk (since some decision makers might be more appropriately invested in the outcome than others, in ways that better serve the value chain). For instance, a store manager might know better than a corporate manager the preferences of local consumers. (For the innovative fashion firm, Zara—which we discuss in chapter 2—part of the job of a local store manager is to discover what customers want that Zara doesn't yet carry.) Consequently, choosing one manager over another to decide what items to stock in what quantities will have different implications for the business model. Delegating decisions to the best-informed party or to the party better able to tolerate associated risks will help reduce inefficiencies.

For example, Amazon, in its early days, ran an essentially stockless fulfillment process by delegating its selection decisions about what books to carry in inventory to a wide network of wholesalers and publishers. Its "sell all, carry few" credo allowed it to tap a limitless virtual inventory, where the costs of carrying such a vast assortment were borne, collectively, by Amazon's suppliers.

The *Why*

The design of a business model typically imposes certain goals and incentives on decision makers. Because decision makers are generally rational actors, these factors can powerfully influence the decisions they make. For instance, an organization that cares mainly about near-term profits will make decisions very different from those of an organization that cares most about long-term sustainability. Or an organization that bears most of the cost but enjoys only a fraction of the rewards derived from a certain investment is unlikely to decide to proceed with it. When differently motivated decision makers must collaborate to create value, incentives have to be adjusted so that the parties can pursue their objectives without damaging the value chain. Understanding the respective parties' incentives helps induce decisions that best create value; it is likewise an aid to identifying misalignments that need repair. The *why* of every key decision has dramatic implications for its business impact.

For example, in an effort to modify incentives, some companies have begun to directly provide certain health-care services to their employees. By integrating doctors, hospitals, and payers into a single organization, they are trying to align all parties around goals to improve health outcomes and exert more control over rising costs. To date, a number of company-run clinics focused on employee wellness have achieved productivity benefits far exceeding the costs of providing the services.

Changing one or more of these four decision levers can transform a business model so that it delivers dramatically superior performance (see figure 1-1). The four W's anchor our framework because they are the innovator's focal point for programmatically identifying BMIs that limit the inefficiencies caused by the harmful impact of both characteristic types of risk and thereby unlock new value.

Suppose a customer purchases complex services (from a doctor or lawyer) or decides whether to buy certain kinds of new products (say, a new-generation energy-saving lightbulb). The customer experiences information risk; he or she doesn't know if the product or service will fulfill his or her needs. This risk occurs, particularly, with products incorporating new technology that is relatively untested, not well understood, and still evolving. Whatever the technology, as long as the decision of what to buy is in the hands of the customer, the information risk can lead to potential inefficiencies and the status quo (the old technologies) will dominate the market.

This is where the *who* lever can change the balance: by putting decisions into the hands of the parties who are

FIGURE 1-1

Inefficiencies, decisions, and the four W's

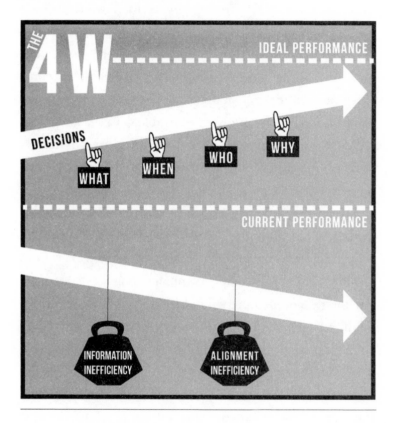

best able to tolerate high information risk or have the most to gain from doing so are among the various types of innovation described in our framework. For instance, if a company itself is hesitating to replace electrical devices in the office with more energy-efficient options, a third party might come in and, instead of selling the customers efficient light bulbs, might sell the customers a reduction in their electricity bill. In this case, technology acquisition itself is managed by the third party that is knowledgeable about different technologies and is therefore more comfortable making these decisions. At some point, presumably, the technology stabilizes and its cost declines; consumers then become more comfortable with the lower risk of adoption. (Chapter 5 looks at the intriguing dynamics of *who* innovations and the example of energy-efficiency service companies.)

Sometimes you may find ways not only to reduce information risk, but also to make the information you are acquiring more useful and better coordinated. LiveOps, an innovative call-center company, has developed an amazingly clever strategy for "hiring," in real time, highly qualified agents (all of whom work from home) and precisely matching their capabilities to incoming customers' needs. By syncing multiple streams of information, its IT-powered model makes call-center performance both more responsive and operationally efficient. Consequently, LiveOps doesn't have to do much guesswork about staffing levels or needed skills; nor is the customer likely to be patched through to an agent unqualified to handle her inquiry. (In chapter 4, we will look more closely at *when* innovations, including the LiveOps example.)

The most important thing to understand about our framework is the interrelatedness of business model decisions—seen through the lens of the four W's—and the creation or reduction of inefficiencies caused by information and incentive-alignment risks. Risk isn't bad per se; it can both limit and enable value creation. But it is important not to take on added risk unwittingly. Our key insight is that the four W's framework is a tool you can use to identify and tune both types of risk up or down, sometimes by moving them from the least to the most suitable party to bear them. In some cases, the right modifications will allow you to take greater risks more prudently. In an Archimedean metaphor, imagine making a change to the angle at which the rear stabilizer of a race car is set so that the car becomes more stable in the turns, thus enabling it to take them faster.

The Path We Recommend

The key to successful business model innovation lies in eliminating inefficiencies by changing the four W's of the decisions that lead to them. We propose a business model innovation approach that proceeds with three steps:

1. Identify key decisions of the current business model.

2. Map out risks and inefficiencies that these decisions create in order to identify those that are most consequential.

3. Change the decision pattern associated with consequential decisions to create new, superior business models that defy risks that would otherwise create inefficiencies.

This process begins with an audit of your business models, encompassing steps one and two. To that end, chapter 2 will help you focus on the flaws and opportunities that you may need to address; it will also dig more deeply into the impact of the two risk types. BMI is fundamentally an activity based on constructive skepticism. It requires that you make yourself (and your organization) open to questioning old assumptions. There isn't a business on earth that doesn't inadvertently do something—maybe a lot of things—that wouldn't survive close scrutiny. The audit is therefore an effort to find underlying weaknesses in the way you've been doing business.

In the subsequent four chapters, we look at each of the four W decision levers in detail, using many examples to illustrate ways of leveraging them to reinvent your business models. We have used different examples to highlight the variety of strategies with which you might modify each of the W's. For example, MyFab changed the *when* aspect of its product-assortment decision by resorting to a crowdsourcing system. And, although we focus throughout the book mainly on changes to a single aspect of a business model's decision pattern, it's not uncommon that changing one W can best be accomplished by changing another. In this respect, MyFab's *when* BMI also served as a *who* innovation, since the company's business model replaced its own product-assortment judgment with that of its customers.

Reinventing all four W's is, of course, theoretically possible. For a start-up in a new industry, where the business model is designed from scratch, this could easily be the case. More often than not, however, you will target your BMI efforts at disrupting a business model that already exists. One of the exciting characteristics of BMI is that its lean economics invite experimentation, reducing the overall risk of any innovation initiative. Moreover, the competitive landscape is always changing. Therefore, as you continue to revisit your business models, you will see further opportunities to modify one or another of the decision pattern's aspects. With each such intervention, you will in effect have created a new model with measurably different performance.

In devising the framework, we found a useful model in the discipline of design thinking, which is a form of holistic, human-centered innovation that seeks to dramatically improve the ways in which people and systems interact. Among other things, we have incorporated design thinking's emphasis on rapid prototyping, experimentation, and the value of learning from diverse sources of data. You will see its influence most strongly in chapter 7, where we show how you can apply our BMI framework in practice. The chapter is built around an implementation case study in which prototyping and experimentation played a key role.

The Likeliest Obstacle

Like any transformational activity, BMI will generate resistance as well as excitement. It has this in common with traditional innovation. Every exhilarating breakthrough is a threat to the status quo. And the status quo—being well known and understood—usually has no trouble rallying its defenders against the uncertainties of a new path or product idea. For that reason, you can expect to encounter opposition when you begin kicking the tires of established business models.

It's impossible to overstate how easily businesses can become hostages of their own success, looking to the past for the keys to their futures. That is, of course, the main danger that established companies face once they've become large and complicated. The path of growth becomes self-enforcing, and the structures that support the past can crowd out new possibilities and fresh perspectives.

That said, smart businesses develop ways of questioning what they do. Amazon.com is one of the businesses we write about in several contexts. From the time he founded the company, Amazon CEO Jeff Bezos was aware of the need to counteract the effects of growth-induced calcification. Though Amazon was born as a business model innovation, it has never stopped changing aspects of the founding model's architecture. As you read on, you will learn that Amazon has in recent years substantially reversed the main pillar of its early growth: the "sell all, carry few" model we noted earlier. That strategy enabled a still-small business to command a virtual inventory able to satisfy every taste. But in the years since its founding, Amazon has aggressively expanded its activities and become more knowledgeable than many of the suppliers it once relied on. Its virtual reach has since become real, and the risks it once shunned are now worth taking on.

Turning against founding wisdom takes real courage. Most businesses struggle to do it. But Amazon teaches us that a company can't afford to sentimentalize the icons of its past. Instead, it needs to be able to "selectively forget the past" and destroy its icons without hesitation.[5] It also needs to be disciplined about experimenting and adjusting things. Amazon is rare in having excelled at that.

Your business most likely falls somewhere between Blockbuster and Amazon, and you probably already know that internal resistance will be an obstacle as you try to advance the role of BMI in your organization. Indeed, your efforts may have to factor in a heavy dose of change management and regular bouts of frustration. But we believe that the BMI game is worth the candle. We will help you to get away from the familiar but old paradigm of reinventing products and looking for new markets and into a new paradigm of rethinking the business model. The rest is up to you.

CHAPTER 2

The Business Model Audit

Since it was published in 2007, a book entitled *What Got You Here Won't Get You There* has been on successive annual lists of the best business books.[1] Its subject is how leaders can best adapt to make themselves and their companies more successful. But we find that the book's title also has compelling resonance for the art of business model innovation. As we noted at the end of chapter 1, inventing the future if your perspective is stuck in the past is very difficult. Your business models need to be strong enough to meet the demands of the present, flexible enough to respond to changing near-term conditions, and monitored over time to make sure they position your business to seize the new opportunities that will ensure its competitive future. Achieving the desired level of business model fitness begins with learning how to analyze its current state. In the same way as many founders and CEOs regularly analyze their firm's financial health through financial audits, maintaining fitness of your business models requires periodic, astute audits.

Our mission in this chapter is therefore to show you what to look for in an audit of your existing business models, with the goal of identifying potential innovation opportunities based on eliminating the models' inherent inefficiencies. Large organizations with multiple divisions and/or diverse product lines might have more than one business model. They should consider these as distinct from one another and examine them separately. However, complex organizations—for example, large hospital systems with treatment, research, and teaching missions—might support models that are deeply intertwined and yet seem to be distinct. But because the models are descended from one dominant decision pattern, they should be treated as a single especially complex model.

We begin by further explaining the role the two characteristic risks play in business models. We illustrate how ignoring these risks can lead to a gross miscalculation of business model performance. We then change gears and provide tools for tracking down these risks in your business model. We start by listing the most common symptoms that point to their presence. We next provide intuitive ways to gauge which of the risks in your model are most detrimental to its performance. Finally, in a preview of subsequent chapters, we draw on the innovative fast-fashion model pioneered by Zara, the popular Spanish fashion brand, to demonstrate how you can reduce risk-driven inefficiencies by modifying one of the four W aspects of the decision pattern. As we explained in chapter 1, the four W's are the main levers of business model innovation, allowing you to improve performance by reducing the inefficiencies caused by risk.

In all, the audit process is meant to help you form a clear diagnostic picture of your existing business models in preparation for deciding which decisions to reinvent.

Business Models and Risks

The main goal of every organization is to create value, defined most often as profits, but also sometimes as a social good.[2] Consequently, a business model audit begins with a concise description of precisely how the organization creates value. In the for-profit world, few managers would disagree that every business needs to know what its *profit formula* is. (Indeed, some businesses use the term "profit formula" interchangeably with "business model.") Although, at the peak of internet boom, people argued that only revenues or "eyeballs" mattered—with profits to somehow follow in the future—most companies that tried to circumvent the profit formula met their demise. The typical profit formula consists of three parts, as shown in figure 2-1.[3]

FIGURE 2-1

The classic profit formula

Revenue model	Cost structure	Resource velocity
Price	Direct, indirect costs	Rate of value output
Volume (market size)	Economies of scale and scope	Lead times, turns, throughput, utilization
Ancillary sales		

The profit formula is largely self-explanatory: the firm receives revenues (price times number of units sold); incurs costs (materials, labor, and machinery); and utilizes resources to different extents (such as spending $10 per hour on an employee who is busy, on average, only 50 percent of the time). This profit formula might be innovated in a number of relatively simple ways:

- Change the revenue model from *pay-per-service* to *subscription* (the difference between iTunes' payment per song and Spotify's monthly fee for unlimited songs).

- Change the revenue model by going up-market (like Renova, the upscale European toilet paper brand); or go down-market (like Tata Motors' Nano, the world's cheapest car). In both cases, the company would adjust the cost structure appropriately.

- Simply reduce the cost structure by offshoring to a low-cost country or even consider entirely virtualizing the business, as many companies have done over the past twenty years.

- Increase the productivity of resources, either by doing more with the same resources or by doing the same things with less. This productivity is typically achieved through process optimization and process reengineering techniques or simply by targeting additional sources of demand.

While all of these potential innovations are legitimate opportunities to improve business models, they are not necessarily game changing. Companies in almost every industry have already tried one or more of them; these innovations are better thought of as low-hanging fruit. And, being familiar, they are easy to imitate, making their advantages rarely sustainable in the long run.

So, although a profit formula like the one discussed is good to have, it lacks something that is important and defining about every business model. What's missing is an *explicit consideration of risks*. Indeed, what realistic organization can, with any precision, describe its revenue structure or cost structure a year in advance? What about three years in advance? Given all the uncertainties inherent in demand, supply, the actions of other firms, product quality, labor availability, the rate of adoption of products, and technology evolution, it becomes harder and harder to make reliable predictions. Perhaps businesses in industries with a very stable customer and supplier base can do a little better, but even those firms are subject to uncertainty about competitors' moves, channel partner actions, and government interventions.

As we noted in chapter 1, we focus on information risk and incentive-alignment risk in particular because they are the two key inefficiency creators in business models, arising because of decision patterns. These two risks are responsible for most, if not all, problems with existing business models. Next we will clarify what they are and how they influence business model performance.

Information risk is a consequence of uncertainty. Many managers base business decisions on incomplete or incorrect information. That's because managers often make decisions long before they have the information to make them *with confidence*. For example, in the pharmaceutical industry, because new drugs take eight to ten years to develop, test, and approve, R&D groups must try to predict not only which diseases to target, but which of the many research lines or treatment approaches is likely to lead to a breakthrough. Similarly, a hospital makes decisions on investments in highly paid specialists and expensive equipment without reliable information about the mix and number of patients it will serve in the future. In such scenarios, misplaced bets are enormously costly. And, as we saw earlier, customers also face information risks that cause models to operate inefficiently. (Unlike incentive-alignment risks, which typically arise *only* when multiple self-interested parties converge, information risks occur even in the absence of multiple actors.)

There is really only one way of reducing information risk to zero: by structuring your business model to wait for complete information. However, most businesses don't have that luxury. The best they can hope for is to close the gap between wild guessing and knowing.

Incentive-alignment risk drives conflict between parties that must collaborate to create value. Business models incorporate incentives that can clash and impede the achievement of common goals. That is because businesses (and their employees) often make decisions on the basis of self-interest rather than what best serves the goals of an entire value chain. This type of risk is therefore context dependent: incentives that motivate excellent performance within the context for which they were designed often cause problems when multiple differing motivations converge. For example, to a surprising (and perhaps mutually amplifying) degree, perversely misaligned incentives within the US housing sector contributed to the 2008 financial crisis as mortgage lenders, mortgage brokers, investment banks, ratings agencies, real estate agents, and home buyers all behaved in wholly self-interested ways.

Learning to identify misalignments and intervene to eliminate the inefficiencies they cause is important. The trick is to get all the parties' incentives aligned with the interests of the value chain as a whole. In the case of

Blockbuster, movie studios had set an inefficiently high price for each VHS tape they sold into the video-rental market. Because the studios had an insufficient stake in the rental-business value chain, they had little reason to care whether Blockbuster lost money, broke even, or turned a profit. Only after Viacom's CEO Sumner Redstone changed the *why* of the pricing decision—by proposing an attractive revenue-sharing deal—were the studios properly incented to care about the downstream outcome.

Incentive-alignment risks can also be dangerously complicated. The more fragmented your supplier relationships, the more important it is to monitor risks caused by misaligned incentives. For example, many offshore suppliers are intensely focused on being lowest-cost producers. This focus may tempt them to resort to illicit practices such as the use of child labor or the operation of unsafe workplaces, whose tragic consequences we saw in the deadly building collapse in Bangladesh in April 2013. Such practices are certainly never in the interests of a valuable brand. Therefore, it is imperative to ensure that, throughout your value chain, you align incentives to produce the outcomes you intend and guard against the ones you don't. As we will describe in chapter 6, the business model of famed intermediary Li & Fung is devoted to aligning the interests of a vast network of global suppliers with those of multinational corporations that purchase their services through *why* innovation.

The Math of Getting Risk Wrong

Factoring in these two types of risk begins to open your eyes to the inefficiencies they cause. Let's consider the celebrated example of Michael Dell, the founder of Dell Computers. With his fledgling computer company, and working out of his University of Texas dorm room, Dell famously transformed the computer industry of the 1980s by turning a make-to-stock model into a make-to-order one. His innovation was to manufacture computers only after the customer placed an order.

In the computer industry of the day, however, the prevailing model was to decide on an assortment of computers of different configurations; then decide, based on estimated demand, how many of each configuration to manufacture; then stock them and wait for the customers to show up. Each configuration was a small problem in business math. Let's say, hypothetically, that you proposed to sell a particular computer for $1,000 with a 50 percent gross margin—meaning that the necessary parts and labor cost $500. You didn't know what the exact demand would be, but you estimated—using averages of past sales—that a thousand customers would want to buy it. So you bought the parts and assembled a thousand computers, at a total cost of $500,000.

Then what? The profit formula would tell you that you could expect to earn $500,000, which is $500 on each of a thousand computers. But it didn't factor in the risk of unpredictable demand. How far away from the demand projection could actual performance get? Very far indeed.

In reality, a demand forecast is no more than an educated guess. There is no certainty of attracting a thousand customers who want this particular computer. Because predictions of demand for new products are so uncertain, let's estimate a 50 percent chance of *no demand at all* for the configuration you assembled, and a 50 percent chance that the product would be so popular that demand would be *twice as high as expected*, with an unforeseen two thousand customers showing up. On average, the demand forecast would be one thousand, which is accurate. But now if demand turned out to be nonexistent, you'd have lots of unsold computers and a loss of $500,000. And if two thousand customers showed up, you'd make a profit of $500,000 on the one thousand computers in stock, but you would disappoint—and probably lose—the one thousand more customers than were in your forecast. In the end, you'd have an equal chance of either losing or earning $500,000. This business model would therefore deliver an *average* profit of zero. And that's before factoring in the lost goodwill of a thousand disappointed extra customers.

This admittedly simplified math sums up the problem of demand forecasting that plagued computer retailing before Michael Dell revolutionized the industry. Dell tackled information risk head-on. As he described in his memoir, the make-to-order model had a clear advantage: "While other companies had to guess which products their customers wanted, because they build them in advance of taking the order, we knew—because our customers told us *before* we built the product. While other companies had to estimate which configurations were the most popular, we knew."[4]

Applying our earlier forecasting math to Dell's make-to-order model, the company would build *no* computers when no customers came (earning zero profit), but it would build two thousand computers (earning a profit of $1 million) when its offering ended up being popular. The Dell model produces an average profit of $500,000, with zero disappointed customers. Notice how dramatically misleading a business model built on averages can be when it fails to account for risk. With average revenue of $1,000 per computer, average cost of $500 per computer, and average demand of a thousand computers, one might expect both the traditional and the Dell models to make the same $500,000, on average. But in reality, the traditional model has an equal chance of either losing or earning $500,000, whereas the Dell model has an equal chance of breaking even or earning $1 million.

By addressing the destabilizing effect of risk, Dell's model accounts for what was missing from the conventional calculation. Dell—having recognized the difficulty of accurately forecasting buyers' exact configuration desires—instead took information risk down to zero. He did so by changing the *when* aspect of the configuration and manufacturing decisions. Thus, a more accurate profit formula would factor in the inherent risks of demand forecasting. You can see that the traditional model is rife with information risk, provides lower average returns, and carries a significant chance of losing money. At worst, Dell's model breaks even.

This simple example leads us to propose the following profit formula redesign (see figure 2-2), which factors in risk sensitivity—the foundation of our innovation approach.

Factoring into the profit formula the riskiness of revenues, costs, and resource velocity highlights a number of powerful new, nonobvious levers you can use to innovate existing business models. Further, we expect that in an

FIGURE 2-2

The new profit formula

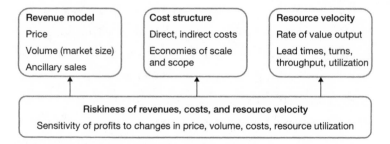

increasingly volatile business environment, more and more industries will achieve significant and inimitable competitive advantages that arise from applying a different risk model, rather than different cost, revenue, or resource-capability models. It is therefore important that any systematic design or improvement of a business model start with a search for the apparent and the not-so-apparent risks in your business model.

Tracking Down Risks in Your Business Model

Risks and their consequent inefficiencies are not shy in announcing their presence. The damage they cause is at times apparent in well-recognized pain points—phenomena that drive down demand, margins, sales, and asset utilization, or just lead to waste. At other times, the impacts of risks on your business model are apparent only as wild variations in performance, which is often misconstrued as good or bad fortune. A comprehensive audit of business models should start with a systematic search for evidence of value lost to risk-driven inefficiencies. We recommend that you start by asking if your organization has experienced any of the most common symptoms that point to the presence of risks in the business model. (See the sidebar "Risk Warning Signs.") The presence of one or more of these symptoms is a strong indicator that

Risk Warning Signs

Some clear indications of the damage that information and incentive-alignment risks can inflict are:

- Frequent dramatic departures from budgeted performance metrics (sales, resource utilization, and so on).

- Wide variations in year-to-year performance.

- High exposure to prices and actions out of the firm's control (for instance, energy prices, partners' behavior).

- Vulnerability of business performance to a few high-impact decisions subject to significant uncertainty.

- Lengthy, complicated forecasting and planning procedures.

- Business models that have not been revisited for a long time so that some decisions are made based on no other logic than habit.

- Frequent inventory write-downs, large stocks of unsold goods, heavy discounting of products or services.

value-destroying inefficiencies are eating away at the performance of your business model.

For example, in November 2006, Nintendo surprised gamers and analysts of the multibillion-dollar video game business with the release of the iconoclast game console,

- Lost revenues owing to insufficient supply, capacity, resources, employees, and so on.

- Expensive, frequently underutilized assets.

- Failure to efficiently use pertinent information in the value chain when making decisions.

- Failure to adopt technology or business practices widely accepted as advantageous.

- Lack of effective measures for assessing partner and employee performance (even when partners and employees score well on performance metrics, the organization suffers).

- Mismatch between consequences the firm faces and those faced by partners or employees.

- Decisions succeed in the short term but damage the firm in the long term.

- Frequent conflict between the firm and its partners.

Once you've noted these inefficiencies, track them back to their root causes, which will often be either (or both) of our two flavors of risk.

the inclusive sounding Wii. While Sony and Microsoft had packed their contemporary consoles with all the ammunition to win the specs battles, Nintendo took a decidedly different tack by developing a console that would extend the market for game consoles well beyond specs-obsessed hard-core gamers. The launch was followed by months of long waits, lines, and a healthy premium in the secondary market on eBay, all phenomena now customary in the first few weeks of any successful consumer electronic launch.[5]

While the initial shortages gave the Wii an allure of desirability and exclusivity, these shortages persisted years beyond the launch, well beyond any rational strategy of deliberate shortage would advise. Many months after the launch, when all the shortage hype had died down, James Lin, a senior game console industry analyst at the MDB Capital Group in Santa Monica, California, opined, "It's staggering." By his estimates, Nintendo was leaving $1.3 billion on the table. "They could easily sell double what they're selling," he commented.[6] To be sure, at this point, no one believed that a deliberate shortage of Wiis would pay dividends later in terms of additional sales, brand building, and so on. In fact, game consoles follow the economics of the classic razor, so that most of the money is made on selling the consumable, in this case, the game title, where just sales of a couple of titles might earn a higher margin than the whole console itself. Why would Nintendo systematically undersupply the market and reduce opportunities for sales of game titles and reduce the attractiveness of its platform to game developers? Given the limitless checkbooks of Nintendo's competition, and the limited time left in the lifetime of this console generation, it was even more urgent for Nintendo to grab market share and lock in consumers when the sun was shining bright. Despite near-consensus among outside analysts, Nintendo management refused to admit any mistakes and was compensated handily for the continuing "strong" sales and high operational efficiency achieved by the organization.

Lurking behind the sometimes heated discourse between external analysts and representatives of Nintendo shareholders and Nintendo management was a symptom of an inefficiency whereby the organization was leaving money on the table and compromising its long-term survival, but the management felt increasingly happy with its strategy.

The path to reinventing business models will often require you to take a symptom and interrogate and torture it till it reveals its root causes. We find that the "five whys" deductive question-answer technique, which the greatest of all Japanese inventors, Sakichi Toyoda, favored, is often fruitful in unraveling the source of the symptom.[7] Behind these symptoms and pain points lie decisions that are made with incomplete information and/or poor incentives.

As the investor pressure and external scrutiny on Nintendo grew, the symptom started revealing more about what was going on. The root cause was probably hidden in the incentives and compensation structures at Nintendo (and most other similar organizations). It turned out that the managers in the Nintendo operations unit responsible for controlling the availability and supply of game consoles were primarily compensated on measures of operational efficiency and financial performance as reported in public statements, such as cash flow, so the company kept inventory to the minimum. Selling all that inventory was an excellent way to keep operational efficiency and margins high. Deliberately limiting supply to ensure that this was always the case meant that management could always meet its targets for efficiency and bottom-line performance. Further, the unexpectedly high interest in the Wii ensured that top-line growth was also in line with targets set for management, based on predictions. What the compensation system did not incentivize as much was the extent of current and, more importantly, future top-line growth that could have been achieved with this once-in-a-lifetime blockbuster product. Not surprisingly, management took the short-term safe strategy, making sure that there was limited supply and corresponding high efficiency, even if this compromised the long-term prospects. At heart, when compensation systems incentivize managers to undertake actions that are not aligned with maximizing the value created by the value chain, an alignment inefficiency is created.

Nintendo is not unique in either showing symptoms of risks and inefficiencies or failing to map the symptoms to their root causes. Only a systematic search for symptoms can help you and your organization honestly identify value-destroying pain points and pinpoint their root-cause inefficiencies.

We hope to next empower you with tools that will turn these inefficiencies into innovation opportunities. But, before we get there, we need to pick our battles with the most worthy of adversaries. We need to get a better measure of the impact of different inefficiencies and identify the battles worth fighting.

Gauging Inefficiencies

There are distinctively different methods for estimating the consequences of the two types of risk.

Incentive-alignment risks—whether they occur within a single firm or between multiple firms—arise when incompatible incentives create self-interested conflicts between *intended* and *actual* objectives. In other words, they produce inefficiencies in your value chain by causing it to pull against itself unproductively.

How can you assess this type of risk? First identify the key players involved in making the decisions that lead to the symptoms and pain points you have identified in the first steps of your audit. For each of these significant decisions, measure the extent of the gap between the intended outcomes and what the real-world outcomes have produced. In other words, how far are the outcomes made in the real world removed from outcomes in an ideal world where all decisions were made by an altruistic decision maker who only cared about maximizing the total value created by the economic system?

Another good way to identify potential incentive-alignment risks is to look at what motivates the key decision makers. List their dominant objectives (what their incentives compel them to value most highly). Then ask some interesting questions: How do the objectives of one decision maker differ from those of another? If the two were brought together in a collaborative effort, how would those differences lead to business model inefficiencies? What could you do to resolve the differences?

Typically, there are just these two contributing factors, just discussed, that drive the extent of incentive inefficiency: (1) the gap between the dominant objectives of different players, and (2) the importance of the decision in question. If you make decisions that are crucial to the strategic direction of your company with misaligned incentives, the consequent incentive inefficiency is likely to be more harmful and a worthy adversary to take on.

Information risk is always present to some extent in every business model. Reducing it is most urgent where the inefficiencies it causes are most intense. Getting an assessment of the extent of information inefficiency involves understanding three key properties of the decision that is made with insufficient information. First is the consequence of the decision. If the decision involves billion-dollar investments, any information inefficiency associated with this decision will evidently be more damaging than the one with an insignificant decision. Second is the degree of reversibility or finality of the decision. Decisions that cannot be easily overturned or revoked (like building a billion-dollar oil rig in the absence of oil) are associated with the highest inefficiency. Last and perhaps most important is a measure of the known unknowns associated with the decisions. Decisions for which you realize there is lot that you don't know are likely to be prime hot spots of information inefficiencies. Often, the degree of known unknowns is closely related to the time between when you make a decision and when information relevant to the decision will be available to you.

For example, in the fashion industry, there are typically only a few competitively important decisions in a given season: designing the collection and planning the assortment; sourcing manufacture (selecting the supplier and country); deciding on transportation mode and order quantity; setting prices; and discounting unsold inventory at the end of the selling season. The consequences for getting a decision wrong range from minor to disastrous. Among this small group of critical decisions are those that drive the fundamental—and most costly—inefficiencies of the industry's current business model. For an apparel retailer that caters to a trendy, fashion-sensitive market, perhaps designing the collection and planning the assortment are most critical.

Next come the reversibility and the measure of known unknowns. While pricing, choice of transportation, and even quantity decisions might be adjusted as information comes in, changing the key design elements might not be easy. The design and assortment decisions also have the highest number of known unknowns. Customer preferences and what styles or fashions catch on are almost as hard to predict as where the next super-hit cute kitty video on YouTube will come from. Last season's trends may be this season's bugaboos. Apparel industry insiders often joke, "Show me this season's peacock, and I will show you next season's feather duster." In addition, the design and assortment decision is also the one made first—the farthest away in time from sales, where the true information on customer preferences becomes available. The consequences—irreversibility and the vast number of unknowns—make the design and assortment decision the ultimate information inefficiency hot spot in this industry.

Follow Risks to Find the Right W

The next question is how to go from recognizing the impact of risks on business model performance to knowing which levers to push in order to innovate and create a superior business model. Let's look at how Zara dealt with the inefficiencies related to information risk.

If you had been performing a business model audit in a fashion firm prior to Zara's key innovation, you might or might not have thought to question the widespread industry practice of making high-stakes bets in June about what customers will want to buy the following March. As our assessment of information inefficiencies shows, it is these bets on different styles and trends that are the biggest sources of information inefficiency.

Compare the fashion industry problem with that of computer makers. Both industries are characterized by high-velocity change; clothing styles and computer capabilities quickly become obsolete. Few buyers want last year's fashion or a computer built around a last-generation microprocessor. As a result, unsold inventory ends up being either deeply discounted or written off. And predictive long-range bets on customer taste can easily miss the mark. For an example of how the traditional business model ratchets up the risk quotient, see what happened to Marks & Spencer, one of Zara's competitors, despite its 130 years of experience in the apparel industry:

Convinced that grey and black would be in fashion during the 1998/1999 season, M&S developed its entire Fall/Winter collection around these two colors. Due to the lead times in its traditional value chain, M&S had to make this decision fully one year in advance of the season. Regrettably, they lost their bet: Both colors proved not to be in fashion that season . . . As was reported in *Businessweek*, "M&S has slashed prices on $1B in goods in an 'Autumn Values' campaign, the biggest off-season sale in its history."[8]

Zara's strategy for overcoming this potentially damaging risk was to innovate its business model by changing the *who* and the *when* of deciding which styles and colors of clothing to offer its customers. It redesigned its business model—and the cost structures, management processes, and manufacturing and logistics arrangements that support it—so that decision making about customer tastes could be done not six to nine months in advance but a mere two weeks before its clothing hit the racks. To do so, Zara had to move decision-making power from the central office planners, who were far removed from customer tastes, to frontline store managers.

Although some components of Zara's cost structure are more expensive than those of competitors (for example, it produces a large proportion of its clothing in Europe and delivers most of it by plane), its fast, local production system—and its empowerment of local store managers to provide input on design and assortment decisions—allows it to predict demand and design and produce fashion only a couple of weeks before selling it. As a result, it is able to continuously adjust its clothing line to reflect new and more reliable information about what customers really want. This allows it to operate with far greater certainty. In fact, the higher costs of Zara's local production are more than offset by the greater accuracy of its fashion bets, which lead to fewer disappointed customers and almost no unsold goods.

Zara doesn't do commercial advertising, a practice unheard of in the fashion industry. Yet, simply by changing the *when* and *who* of design and assortment decisions, Zara has given its customers good reasons to be continuously interested in making frequent visits to Zara websites and stores: because they will always see something new. Could it be that newness is addictive to the point of making advertising superfluous?

When we spoke to Jesus Eschevarria, chief communications officer of Zara's parent company Inditex, he summarized the firm's thinking: "Don't talk about yourself. It is the customer who should talk about you." Certainly, Zara accepts a degree of added brand risk by forgoing advertising, but that risk is more than compensated for by the constant newness of its assortment. The traditional fashion business model, on the other hand, faces the challenge of renewing depleted customer interest three or four times a year, which requires spending heavily on advertising. Zara can spend its marketing budget in other ways.

In that sense, the fast-fashion *when* innovation supported by *who* innovation becomes a virtuous circle. Not surprisingly, others in the fashion industry are now following suit, reducing information inefficiencies in pursuit of a host of potential benefits.

The point of conducting a business model audit is to prepare you to reinvent existing business models or create entirely new ones. That work is the subject of the coming chapters. Each of the decision pattern's four W levers has its own chapter. For each lever, we will describe three distinct innovation approaches and the conditions under which they are appropriate. By the end of chapter 6, we will have outlined a dozen varieties of business model innovation that you can accomplish by changing the decision pattern. For example, we would describe Zara's innovation as *changing the* when *of the "design and assortment" decision to delay it as much as possible, while also changing the* who *to delegate decisions to the party with the most information.* These are just two of the dozen approaches to BMI innovation that we describe in detail in the coming chapters.

As you go through the business model audit, remember that auditing is a journey, not an event. Don't think of the audit as a onetime deal or an activity reserved for a crisis. Instead, view it as a regular opportunity to assess your firm's overall strategic hygiene. Use it to identify developing problems or potential new businesses—

conditions that may not need immediate action but bear watching over time. Prioritize a pipeline of BMI initiatives: some urgent, some for midrange development, some for the far horizon, and some that have been completed and whose results should be evaluated. We are sure that you—like Zara—will unearth the inefficiencies that afflict your own business model through a thorough audit. Once you've identified the decisions associated with them, you will be at the very center of the BMI universe, where your best opportunities to eliminate the most damaging inefficiencies are clustered. There will be plenty for you to work with.

TAKEAWAYS

Look carefully for the symptoms. Symptoms of inefficiencies may be apparent to all or may be hiding behind the guise of fate, the established way of doing business, or other excuses. Question the assumption and don't let any symptoms and pain points escape unnoticed.

Interrogate the symptoms. Symptoms may disguise themselves in various forms. Keep questioning till you arrive at the root cause of the pain point and can attribute it to either information or alignment inefficiency.

Follow the money. The most promising opportunities are clustered around inefficiencies associated with high-consequence decisions made with the greatest misalignment between actual and ideal incentives, decisions that are hard to go back on, and decisions that involve many known unknowns.

CHAPTER 3

The *What* Strategy

Organizations typically fail to recognize that adopting a different set of decisions can dramatically transform the business model, even if all else remains unchanged. Thinking back to the physics of Archimedes' lever, we know that relatively small exertions can produce large results. For example, consider what happened to the rental-car business model when Zipcar chose to rent by the hour instead of by the day. For Zipcar, a cascade of strategic and operational differences flowed from that choice, but it was still fundamentally in the business of renting cars to customers who needed them temporarily.

In a different industry, IBM left behind its guise of "heavy iron" hardware manufacturer in the mid-1990s and remade itself as an IT services provider for the internet age. Though the company never stopped developing innovative technologies, it learned to see itself and its customer mission in a new light. Getting to that point required questioning many of the bedrock assumptions that had long guided—some would say calcified—its strategy, its culture, and the way it was viewed in the marketplace. IBM realized that changing aspects of the way a business defines itself can lead in surprising new directions.

This chapter is about the decisions that define the problems your business model most aggressively sets out to solve—what the business is about and what its attitudes are on questions of risk.

Firms tend to take for granted their foundational decisions, giving little thought to the impact they may have on business model inefficiencies. Thus, the long-established levers that organizations use to achieve their goals persist for reasons of historical habit or because they are the natural, widely accepted practices of a given industry. For instance, the dominant model in the rental-car business is to rent for periods of one or more days; and most companies use promotions and discounts to push renters to lease by the week. Although Avis's acquisition of Zipcar has yet to play out, it may in time initiate a wider questioning of at least that element of industry bedrock.

So, if you were to stop and think about it—as you will when you conduct your business model audit—you will recognize that various levers are at a firm's disposal, each imposing dramatically different kinds and degrees of inefficiency. Some trigger a reliance on inadequate information; some create misalignments with respect to the organization's objectives and incentives or to those of its customers and channel partners; and still others turn on more fundamental aspects of the business, such as its orientation to risk of all types. Is it comfortable embracing risky decisions, or does it prefer to eliminate risk from consideration as much as possible? No organization, however, should take on any risk unwittingly. And there may be instances when reducing your exposure to information and incentive-alignment risks allows you to take on more risk in other categories. (Recall, for example, how Zara's ability to delay design-and-assortment decisions allowed it to tolerate higher supply-chain costs.)

In the three following sections, we will look at the trade-offs associated with choosing what decisions the firm should be making, primarily with the objective of balancing risks with returns. We will therefore show the effect on business model performance (in terms of reduced inefficiencies and enhanced value) that results from modifying those key decisions.

First, we will consider how the organization can dramatically innovate through *focus*: deciding either to narrow the scope of its activities (perhaps by doing one thing exceptionally well) or to make decisions associated with minimal information risk (manufacture black socks instead of stylish dresses). Then we will highlight another strategy for tilting the business model toward *fewer, lower-risk decisions,* sometimes with the goal of support-ing greater risk in other areas. Finally, we will look at innovations that *hedge the consequences* of one decision against those of another, with the goal of mitigating their information and/or incentive-alignment risks. In this ap-proach, the goal is to select decisions in such combinations as to mutually compensate, rather than amplify, their re-spective risks, or to creatively pool the decisions of mul-tiple organizations, thus spreading their risks across mul-tiple participants.

Focusing the Scope of Key Decisions

As everyone knows, Amazon thrives in large part because of a highly efficient supply chain management strategy that allows it to quickly deliver millions of reasonably priced products to customers. However, in October 2010, *Bloomberg Businessweek* ran a cover story with the sen-sationalistic headline, "What Amazon Fears Most."[1] The article wasn't about Google, Facebook, eBay, or some other internet titan. The headline ran over a picture of a diaper-wearing infant, appropriate because the article pro-filed a relatively small New Jersey–based internet start-up called Quidsi—Latin for "what if." Quidsi, cofounded by Marc Lore, formerly a student in one of our classes at the Wharton School of Business, was best known for its main venture, online retailer Diapers.com.

Unlike Amazon, which diversified aggressively from books to become an online retailer of just about everything, Diapers.com was distinctive for its radical embrace of focus in choosing what products to carry and hence what decisions to make. Internet retailers make many decisions, but most of them are driven by that one fundamental choice. Founded in 2005 (while Lore was still a student), Diapers.com lived up to its name: it sold only baby-care consumables—diapers, wipes, infant formula, diaper-rash ointments, talcum powder, and so on. By 2010, its revenues hit $300 million, and it was far outselling Amazon in the category. Whether Amazon ($32 billion in revenues) "feared" Diapers.com is a matter for speculation, but the start-up was definitely on Amazon's radar. Not long after the *Businessweek* article, Amazon acquired Quidsi for $550 million. What attracted Amazon's interest was the strength of a business model innovation achieved through *sharp focus*.

Focus affords some unique advantages. For one thing, having a narrow product offering reduces the information risk associated with deciding questions of assortment or selection and demand. Compared to Amazon, Quidsi/Diapers.com managed relatively few stock-keeping units (SKUs). Amazon, on the other hand, prides itself on selling absolutely everything. It must therefore make myriad decisions related to forecasting product demand, selecting suppliers, managing inventories, and adjusting prices for every single product it sells. The decision pattern associated with each of these products leads to risks that the company must take pains to manage. Among its vast assortment are products that differ widely in margins and in the variability of customer demand. Products with high margins and stable demand provide high returns with low risks; they are the most desirable products in Amazon's portfolio, often subsidizing other products with higher demand variability or lower margins. (Even though Amazon began life with a single product category, it chose one characterized by exceptional breadth and demand variability. But compared to early days, it now must manage a risk profile of extraordinary amplitude and diversity.)

The early success of Diapers.com—from zero to $300 million in revenues in five years—was achieved because of, not in spite of, focus. Nonetheless, on the surface, diapers and other baby consumables might appear to be a terrible product to sell on the internet. Diapers are bulky and expensive to ship. And they have low margin because *everyone*—from convenience stores to Costco—sells them. Conventional business model thinking, which looks only at costs and revenues, would declare diapers unsellable online.

But diapers do have a few things going for them. Demand is highly predictable; infants pee and poop constantly over an extended period of time. And product variety is quite limited; there are only three or four major diaper manufacturers, and diapers come in just a handful of sizes. Given that every newly acquired customer will use the product repeatedly for two years or more, you can count on—excuse our pun—a solid stream of revenues with little or no risk for a long time to come. Consequently, the challenge of predicting demand for diapers is orders of magnitude smaller than for most other products. As a category, baby-care consumables pose a nearly trivial level of information risk. And even though diapers are the category's low-margin "anchor tenant," the ointments, powders, wipes, and other related SKUs drive higher margins.

Focus was also a powerful ally in helping Diapers.com solve its supply chain issues. Perhaps you have noticed the empty space inside many Amazon packages. Such a waste! Diapers.com achieves nearly zero packaging waste with an order-picking and -packing process assisted by robots and software. The *Businessweek* article notes that the company "has specified 23 different sizes of boxes to ship in, and has designed a software program that knows the dimensions of each ordered product and can fit them into the smallest possible box, which saves on shipping. The boxes are automatically made at the warehouse and delivered to the pickers by the robots."[2]

According to Scott Hilton, another former student of ours at Wharton who served as head of supply chain for Diapers.com and later as a vice president of operations, the degree of risk—from predicting demand to managing supply chain logistics—was exceptionally low because of the company's limited product assortment. Not surprisingly, risk-driven inefficiency proved to be a lot lower for focused Quidsi than for a broad generalist like Amazon. In its product category, Diapers.com was several times more efficient than Amazon. So it's no wonder Amazon decided to acquire its upstart competitor.

Focusing on a narrowly defined set of decisions in order to eliminate multiple information risks can be a very powerful type of business model innovation for industries, such as retailing, that face many variable risks across a diverse assortment of goods. You therefore might not think of a hospital as an institution likely to benefit from the kind of sharp focus that helped Diapers.com succeed. But even in environments known for the complexity of their activities, there is room for specialized focus and simplification.

Some interesting health-care (service) innovations have been built around the premise that the higher quality and efficiency of a focused service provider trumps the versatility and flexibility of a general hospital (meaning a non-specialized institution chartered to serve its patients' every need). Large general hospitals face a wide range of risks (some quite distinct from the two types of risk we've discussed so far), the stakes of which are dramatically higher than those faced in most other industries. The risks fall into four main categories:

- First, there is the purely medical risk of contagion associated with the *interaction of the many patients and procedures* that a general hospital handles.

For example, infectious patients can kill relatively healthy ones. About a hundred thousand people die every year in the United States from infections acquired inside the hospital.[3] Most of these are spread through ventilation systems or caused by improper sanitization and disinfecting procedures. Much of this risk arises from the decision to service any and all patients in the same facility.

• Many information risks result from *variable, highly unpredictable demand*. Emergency rooms, for example, can be overwhelmed by flu epidemics, industrial or highway accidents, or multiple gunshot victims, all on top of the steady flow of uninsured patients who come to the ER for routine medical care. With the variety of illnesses afflicting patients and uncertainty about the service times that each will require, it is difficult to plan for just enough essential resources. There will usually be either too much capacity or too little, a clear symptom of inefficiency.

• *Information flow in a general hospital can be a challenge*, especially around shift changes, leading to characteristic inefficiencies. For example, unless accurate patient status information is exchanged between departing and arriving nurses, elements of care can either fall through the cracks or be duplicated needlessly (sometimes dangerously).

- Finally, *incentive-alignment inefficiencies* sometimes come into play when doctors and others make decisions motivated by reasons other than the patient's best interest (as we will describe in chapter 6).

None of these problems exist at Laastari Lähiklinikka, a chain of small Finnish clinics located in shopping malls and other densely populated areas. The clinics pursue a focused *what* strategy by treating a limited set of the most common illnesses, including allergies, colds, sore throats, flu, and simple infections. They also administer the most common vaccinations. Depending on a patient's needs, the fee for a visit might range between €25 and €45 (the same services would likely cost €100 at a Finnish general hospital). Clinics are open seven days a week, require no appointment, and claim to have earned 100 percent customer satisfaction.

Patient experiences are more predictable in the clinics, where there is lower risk than in a general hospital of coming into contact with virulent infectious diseases. Laastari Lähiklinikka saves on labor costs by having nurses, not physicians, deliver services; and it saves on infrastructure because the clinics don't need expensive diagnostic equipment. (Patients whose needs go beyond what the clinics can provide are, of course, referred to a full-service hospital.) All procedures take ten to fifteen minutes of provider time. This makes workloads predictable and long lines unlikely, which in turn enables staff utilization to approach its theoretical maximum.

Laastari Lähiklinikka is neither unique nor the first such health-care venture to realize the risk-reducing benefits of focus. The US-based MinuteClinic chain has been around since 2000, offering a similar list of limited services provided by nurse practitioners or physician assistants at roughly six hundred centers in CVS pharmacy stores. According to the latest data, MinuteClinic's operating costs were 40 percent to 80 percent lower than in general hospitals, yet the entire chain of clinics broke even in 2010 and has continued to grow (CVS Caremark acquired the chain in 2006).[4]

Focused health-care approaches can do more than administer vaccines or treat cold and flu symptoms. A small Canadian hospital called Shouldice has done nothing but repair abdominal hernias since 1945. Its focus on one particular surgery has allowed it to deliver superior quality at a far lower cost than a general hospital could ever achieve. Yet it offers its doctors and nurses higher salaries than do other hospitals.[5] Although Shouldice is a private hospital in the mainly government-run Canadian medical system, the government happily pays for Shouldice surgeries because they are less expensive than elsewhere. And there is a steady stream of cash-paying US patients who are regularly drawn to Canada by Shouldice's reputation for quality. (Shouldice, after seventy years on its own, was acquired in September 2012 by Toronto-based Centric Health.)

Since hernias are neither life threatening nor thought to be especially complicated, they are often performed by general surgeons. However, since Shouldice operates only on hernias, over time it has perfected a quick and efficient production-line approach. There is just one basic procedure, and Shouldice has standardized it the way Ford standardized automobile assembly a hundred years ago. Moreover, because each doctor performs hundreds of procedures every year, individual surgeons attain high proficiency very quickly. The quality of patient outcomes is consequently also high, with customer satisfaction to match.

Hernia repair is far from being the most complicated procedure a focused hospital can perform. In 2011, *The Economist* honored Indian cardiac surgeon Devi Shetty with an award in the field of business process innovation. The award cited Shetty's Narayana Hrudayalaya Hospital in Bangalore for "reducing health-care costs using mass-production techniques. His hospital performs more heart operations at a lower cost and a lower mortality rate than leading American hospitals." [6] Narayana Hrudayalaya employs forty-two cardiac surgeons who do more than three thousand bypass surgeries per year, along with many other less demanding cardiac procedures. Shetty, like Shouldice, drew inspiration from automobile assembly lines. "Japanese companies reinvented the process of making cars," Shetty told the *Wall Street Journal*. "That's what we're doing in healthcare. What healthcare needs is process innovation, not product innovation."[7]

We are not suggesting that general hospitals are a thing of the past. Many patients suffer from a number of ailments in combination and are best served by large, multi-specialty institutions. Moreover, as we will discuss in chapter 6, not all BMI initiatives in health care are necessarily driven toward focus. But focus can be a powerful strategic lever in any number of industries.

For example, many law firms focus on particular legal specialties, from criminal law to trusts and estates. In the aviation industry, airlines have reaped the benefits of focus by appealing to distinct customer segments: price-sensitive family leisure travelers (AirTran); price-insensitive business travelers (the major US legacy carriers) and high-end leisure travelers (Singapore Airlines, for one); and an international youth market that wants both value and style (Virgin Atlantic, JetBlue). In the ancient history of the fast-food business, the founders of White Castle and Mc-Donald's saw an advantage in focusing on what, at the time, was an unusually limited menu of items. In all of these cases, a change to the decision pattern reduced the complexity of decision making and eliminated some of the risks the businesses faced.

CAVEATS: You must be mindful that narrow focus can leave a firm vulnerable to other kinds of risks. With all or most of your eggs in one basket, a single sudden change in the environment could wreak havoc. Imagine what would happen to Shouldice if a pill that treated hernias were to be introduced tomorrow. If such an admittedly far-fetched breakthrough occurred, Shouldice would be devastated. However, the general hospital would be safely hedged by its widely diversified nature.

Taken together, focused business models work best when they appeal to distinct market segments, each presenting different sets of interests and risks that cannot be easily or effectively addressed by a single business model serving all segments. Consequently, if yours is a business that serves highly diverse segments, it may be best to subdivide one business model into multiples. That allows you to more sharply focus the *what* of your decisions to pursue an opportunity to become—as Shouldice has—the most efficient model for the targeted segment. And, as you have seen, focused approaches enable you to go all in on a single segment (hernia sufferers) or product set (baby-care consumables), achieving far higher certainty about customers' needs and wants through reduced information risk and more predictable demand. (Amazon, having acquired online shoe and apparel retailer Zappos as well as Quidsi, has wisely allowed its focused acquisitions to operate with considerable autonomy in serving their segments. You might think of this as Amazon's virtual version of business model subdivision.)

We turn now from focus to a different *what* modification that nonetheless achieves some of the same benefits: *identifying key commonalities* among customer segments in order to reduce the number of decisions you must make and their consequent impact on risk.

What Beetles and Bugattis Share

As we just saw, reducing the scope of risk-creating decisions that an organization must make is a potent way to build a successful new business model. But the downside is that the company must rely on a single product, service, or customer segment. Focus may also exclude key customer needs (say you have both a hernia and a torn knee ligament, both from lifting a piano, or you would like to buy both diapers *and* beer, a rather natural combination). How, then, can you reduce the number of risky decisions you make while still successfully serving the needs of multiple segments?

The case of Volkswagen offers an interesting example. It may have escaped your notice that Volkswagen quietly passed both General Motors and Toyota in 2011 to become the largest automobile company in the world.[8] So what is its secret?

Because investments in labor, materials, plants, and equipment are so high, automakers feel information risk intensely. Likewise, competition in the automotive industry is fierce, and global manufacturers must tackle a number of mounting problems that add further uncertainty to their business models:

- Unstable demand caused by rising gas prices and other economic disruptions.

- An influx of new competitors from emerging economies.

- Growing pressure from governments to produce greener, more efficient vehicles.

While the big three US auto companies have all recently endured challenging times, Volkswagen has done very well indeed. Its success is all the more remarkable when you realize that VW manufactures 245 different car models marketed under 10 brand names. Across this mix, VW's brands differ dramatically in price and market niche, from the relatively low-cost Volkswagen SEAT to extraordinarily expensive Bugattis and Bentleys.

Volkswagen has always been highly successful in its home region of Western Europe. But now it is also a best-selling manufacturer in China and South America. And its sales grew a whopping 30 percent in the United States in 2012 (as of this writing). While no single reason can account for its performance, we would nominate the careful, centralized risk management approach that VW applies to its very complex business model. Within a huge global business, it has managed to develop an efficient discipline for reducing the number of decisions in an especially complicated organization.

Predicting demand for existing cars is hard enough; predicting demand for the cars of *future* model years is all but impossible. It is easy to make a very costly mistake by betting money on something that does not sell as anticipated. In the automotive industry, such mistakes are extremely expensive: factories and tooling cost hundreds of millions of dollars, and unionized labor is paid whether or not there is demand for the car (though a lack of demand can, of course, lead to lower production, fewer daily shifts, and eventual layoffs). What Volkswagen did was lower the information risk of unpredictable demand by focusing engineering ingenuity on using many of the same basic parts in multiple cars, even cars of different brands.

In a strategy known as both "platform sharing" and "component commonality," decisions are modified so that demand for individual components becomes stable because the information risks associated with predicting demand for any one car are distributed across multiple models and brands. It is far easier to predict aggregate demand for dozens of components than for thousands. Although the number of products the organization offers remains unchanged, the number of underlying decisions—and their associated risks—is reduced tremendously. Just as Lego allows you to create endless variations from a few basic shapes, Volkswagen builds many cars from a few basic platforms. Platform sharing thus became the new *what* that helped reduce the potential for information inefficiencies caused by VW's broad portfolio of brands and selections.

Executing such a strategy would be a relatively easy task if all the cars for which components are common also look and feel the same. But that's not what Volkswagen wanted, for it would have been a recipe for disaster. Few readers are likely to remember a 1983 cover of *Fortune* showing four different GM car makes, from low-end Chevrolet to high-end Cadillac. All four looked roughly identical because of common parts, frames, and body styles (a cookie-cutter impression that was further enhanced by the pictured cars' identical paint jobs). Taking a lesson from the GM experience, Volkswagen made sure that its use of common components would be imperceptible to customers. It thus put distinctive bodies on the different car platforms, while also including a number of common components out of sight.

Depending on whether you pay a premium price for an Audi A6 or a lot less for a Volkswagen Jetta, the fact that they share some innards may seem either brilliant or a rip-off. But it makes for a tremendously profitable business model. Among smaller vehicles (of which VW sells seven million per year), it installs common transmissions, steering assemblies, front axles, and air-conditioning and ventilation systems. Together, these components account for 60 percent of the cost of each car. VW has a similar modularization program for its less numerous larger vehicles.

Reducing the scope of decisions about component options is not the only way automakers have innovated their business models. Manufacturing logistics can also be a lever to gain greater production flexibility under conditions that are both highly variable and dangerously unpredictable.

US automakers traditionally built factories designed to produce only one model of car. For years, this was a reasonable approach because the number of models in the market was quite limited. The life span of an auto factory is from twenty-five to forty years. When any new factory is planned, there is obviously high information risk around the likely long-term demand for particular car models. When the supply of one model exceeds demand, you would expect the factory to cut production. However, a plant's considerable fixed expenses cause the car's per-unit cost to balloon when volume drops. Based on their incentives, plant managers are motivated to keep per-unit cost down, keeping volume up, notwithstanding the low demand. This floods the market with a surplus that quickly leads to deep discounting. (In all, this is a classic incentive-alignment risk.)

Plants can, of course, retool to produce something different, but retooling typically idles a plant for as long as six months, and the cost is quite high: in 2009, Ford spent $550 million to retool a Michigan plant, which formerly manufactured SUVs, to produce the new Ford Focus.

Wouldn't it instead make sense to build facilities that are more flexible in the first place? Japanese manufacturers were pioneers in doing this: designing factories able to produce multiple cars alongside each other on the same production lines. The advantage of such flexibility is the ability to switch production from a model in low demand to one that is selling briskly. While flexible plants are more expensive to build, they minimize the far more costly risk of excess demand or supply. A manufacturer can save billions of dollars down the road on lower discounts, lower inventory carrying costs, and lower overtime compensation—all of which are the familiar pain points of auto industry information risk. Well before US automakers caught on, this strategy helped Japanese automakers become so dominant in their heyday. More recently, their US rivals began investing heavily in manufacturing flexibility.[9]

CAVEATS: It is important to note that, under most circumstances, it costs more to create a decision pattern with fewer consequences. Flexible production facilities are naturally more expensive to build. Likewise, common components cost VW more to produce because they must be engineered for an unusually wide range of performance demands across different makes and models. As you would expect, there are important risk-return calculations to be made before enabling such variability.

A further caveat is that identifying commonalities among different segments of the market and reducing the number of associated decisions will work best when the demand from those segments is not too correlated—meaning that they will not all experience their highs and lows simultaneously—and the cost of establishing flexible designs and production technologies is not too high.

Hedging Your Decisions

A third approach to *what* innovation is to hedge decisions so that they compensate each other's risks. Just as financial institutions create portfolios of investments that, when assembled shrewdly, hedge each other's risks, other kinds of businesses can select the decisions they make so as to reduce the overall riskiness of the business model.

The decision to purchase a plane is invariably made in the face of information risk. There is always considerable uncertainty about passenger demand, which fluctuates based on circumstances that are sometimes beyond any airline's control. On average, airlines fill only about 70 percent of their seats. This problem is largely responsible for the general unprofitability of the entire industry. The bright spots are usually found among airlines such as Southwest in the United States, Ryanair in the United Kingdom, or Jetstar in Australia, each of which has innovated its business model by focusing on a standardized service approach. All three, for example, eliminate decisions and reduce risk by selecting a single cabin configuration and a single aircraft type.

There is, however, another well-performing business model exemplified by Chile's LAN Airlines.[10] LAN prospers in part by creating hedging options for itself. Although doing this effectively increases the number of decisions LAN must make, it does so in a risk-reducing way: the selected decisions compensate for each other's risks.

Like many powerful business model innovations, LAN's hedging strategy is quite simple. Most passenger airlines steer clear of the cargo business. Typical US legacy airlines (US Airways/American, Delta, and United/ Continental) derive no more than 5 percent of their revenues from cargo. Even the few airlines that operate high-volume passenger and cargo services tend to keep them separate (different planes, routes, and schedules). But LAN uses the same wide-body passenger planes, flying international routes, to mix passengers and cargo. International flights often have inflexible schedules that require planes to wait on the ground for extended periods before departing. (Almost all travel from the Americas to Europe is on overnight flights.) LAN turns this wait time into an ancillary revenue opportunity. During the day, in addition to carrying passengers, it becomes a regional cargo operation, delivering time-sensitive shipments—fresh salmon and other perishables from South America to Europe, and expensive electronics in the other direction. A plane to Santiago that has picked up a load of cargo in Europe has time to deliver it to other Chilean cities before returning to Santiago in time for its next overnight flight, likewise loaded with cargo and passengers for European destinations.

This approach makes sense for several reasons, all of which boil down to reducing the information risk that drives underutilized capacity. This inefficiency exists because airlines make capacity decisions infrequently—by ordering new airplanes—and such decisions are hard to reverse. High demand volatility leaves airlines vulnerable to periods of over- and underutilized capacity, with harsh effects on revenue.

Diversification of revenue streams mitigates the revenue-related risks. Hedging passengers with cargo works well because their respective demand curves rarely rise or fall in concert, meaning that information risks are felt less acutely when one or the other of the revenue streams dips.

Moreover, the option of carrying cargo allows the airline to fly profitably with fewer passengers. Thus it can afford to serve destinations that would be unattractive without a "subsidy" from the cargo business. That, in turn, allows LAN to economically fly new routes and expand its presence to cities that other airlines avoid, a further example of how reducing risk in one area can support adding it in another. Even though managing diversified revenue streams increases the number of decisions LAN makes, it coordinates those decisions such that each compensates for the other's risks.

Other BMI hedging approaches are more about pooling decisions than pairing them. Consider, for example, commercial maritime shipping. It is a tricky business characterized by huge cyclicality that is almost always caused by events beyond shipping companies' control. For ship owners, an unregulated market of freight transportation is riddled with risks related to fluctuating demand and prices. In the oil-shipping sector, the price of crude is a key driver of demand and volume. An especially warm or cold winter will either depress or stimulate demand. Likewise, disruptions to refinery capacity will leave some percentage of ships sitting empty. The recent emergence of commercial shipping pools is a way of spreading out the risks. Tankers International LLC (TI) is one of a number of companies that offer the owners of tanker fleets and their customers an option to hedge decisions.[11]

Tankers International (TI) has assembled a pool of tankers from member tanker owners and operators and provides management services for the vessels in the pool (all are from the largest classes of crude oil carriers). Members of the pool share equitably in the demand that Tankers International receives. This reduces the impact of low-demand periods on any single tanker company. TI maximizes each vessel's capacity by, for example, arranging so-called "backhaul" loads, so that a ship delivering cargo to its destination can either reload there or at the next nearest port where a new cargo can be picked up. That way, ships spend less time empty. And when the time comes to invest in an expensive new ship, member tanker owners can place their orders with greater certainty that the pool will help spread out the risk and deliver steady demand.

For customers, access to a large pool of tankers ensures that at least one vessel will have sufficient capacity when the need arises. TI also acts as a logistics partner for some of its largest customers, providing tools that help them manage their shipping activities and inventories.

While the pool approach to matching supply with demand reduces informational risks, it might also give rise to potential incentive-alignment risks. Ship owners need to have an attractive incentive to commit their vessels to the pool and make the aggregate capacity available to customers. Otherwise, there would be no reason to join. Tankers International innovates around this risk through a novel system of pool points, allotted to each vessel according to a formula based on its carrying capacity, speed, and expenses, as measured against a reference voyage.[12] The idea is to ensure that each member of the pool receives a fair share of revenues—neither so big that other ship owners feel cheated nor so small that the company declines to join the pool.[13]

What is interesting about the pool concept is its power to attract members who under most circumstances would consider themselves fierce competitors. However, the volatile nature of the competitive environment is such that a business model that provides a hedge against sharp fluctuations, and the inefficiencies they cause, can make competitors comfortable enough to share in the rewards that come from cooperating.

A now-familiar arrangement similar in spirit to tanker pools emerged in the 1990s in the high-tech industry in the form of electronics contract manufacturing.[14] Some of today's largest contract manufacturers are the muscle behind well-known brands, most notably Apple. But their main value is in serving small firms trying to lower the risk of bringing new products to market. Demand for electronic products is extremely volatile, and many products are short-lived. A small electronics company makes a risky commitment when it builds a manufacturing facility and hires workers. What if demand for the product dwindles quickly or never materializes in the first place?

Contract manufacturers are able to pool the demand from numerous small electronics vendors and make products to their specifications. In this way, they can hedge the decisions of many original equipment manufacturers (OEMs) against one another, driving risk far lower than that which an individual company would face.

CAVEATS: Not all hedging plays are created equal. Ideally, an organization should strive to find decisions for which the risks fully counterbalance each other. For instance, a firm that seeks to sell two products would choose them so that their demand fluctuations are negatively correlated (as a statistician might put it), meaning that demand would be high for one when it was low for the other.[15] Or a maker of seasonal products could seek a hedge allowing it to sell year-round and defy traditional cyclicality. For example, a manufacturer of ski apparel hedges sales in North America with sales in South America, where the seasons are opposite. Overall demand stays fairly constant, and the required production capacity bears lower information risk. However, if events in the environment were to change the nature of the risks (a worldwide recession, perhaps), demand could become positively correlated, making the hedge less effective.

TAKEAWAYS

Determining *what* decisions to select in designing business models is usually the dominant driver of their risks and inefficiencies. Nonetheless, organizations often take these foundational decisions for granted. A few simple rules apply when reinventing the business model by modifying what it defines as important:

Balance focus with flexibility. The so-called Pareto principle applies here: 20 percent of your products or services account for 80 percent of your risks. Eliminate just a few, and the business model will improve disproportionately. If, like Amazon, a wide product and service offering is part of your value proposition, try to make sure you have enough steady volume and higher margin products to offset your higher-risk offerings.

Reduce the number of decisions. It's possible to reduce the number of decisions in your business model without reducing your product or service offerings. Like Volkswagen, you can "Lego-ize" a certain number of key components and share them across platforms. Or you might invest a little more in facilities equipped to flexibly manufacture different products. Either way, the risks of managing broad or complex product lines, subject to volatile demand, can be effectively mitigated.

Hedge decisions against one another. Business risks arising from different decisions seldom rise and fall synchronously. As LAN and other firms have learned, you can leverage complementary decisions to build a portfolio of risks that hold each other in check, balance demand fluctuations, and optimize capacity (making labor and facilities more consistently productive). Sometimes you can also hedge by pooling resources with other companies.

What Innovation in Action: The Housekeeping Industry

Consider an individual or an organization providing residential housekeeping services (maid services). The service provider typically spends almost 20 percent to 30 percent of her workday commuting between different work locations. The provider must either carry heavy commercial equipment and cleaning products from one service location to another or use different small-scale equipment at each location, further slowing him or her down. Finally, there is a setup at each location (drive, change clothes, and so on). What if the provider changed what market she serves? Instead of providing cleaning services to residents in a catchment area that is typically a few square miles, it focuses on providing cleaning services to a hyper-local market—the residents of just one building or one block. Citruz-Up, a start-up conceptualized by some recent participants in one of our innovation programs, is dreaming of doing exactly that. Citruz-Up will provide cleaning services at a 30 percent discount to the prevailing fee to residents of any building or block if more than a specified number of residents sign up to use the service. Not only will the services be cheaper, but there is no minimum number of hours to be booked, customers do not need to provide equipment and consumables, and they can also use multiple value-added services, such as getting their fridge stocked with simple consumables, getting their toilet paper refreshed, and so on. How will Citruz-Up manage to provide such hotel-quality housekeeping services at a lower cost? By innovating what market the provider serves—a focused hyper-local market that eliminates all the inefficiencies associated with commuting, using efficient standardized equipment that the provider can easily carry from one service location to the adjacent next service location, and by having a consolidated stock of consumables at the service location—exactly what housekeeping in a hotel does.

CHAPTER 4

The *When* Strategy

The cliché gets it almost right: timing *is* everything. Actually, timing *and* sequence are everything. Determining when you must make key business model decisions and the order in which they are arranged, relative to one another, is crucially important to your business model's performance and to the value it creates (or destroys). So if you modify the decision pattern to change the absolute timing of key decisions and/or the way they interrelate, you can produce powerful business model innovations.

As we have already seen with Zara, managers, when given enough time, acquire more and better information about the consequences of their decisions. For instance, most business forecasts become increasingly accurate as managers learn more about the business environment. The ability to predict customer preferences and subsequent demand is clearly optimized the longer you can wait before producing goods for sale.

Moreover, the sequence in which managers make their decisions will influence the consequences of those that are made earlier or later, whether within a single firm, a value chain, or an industry. In a value chain, for example, one party's prior decision will powerfully affect the trade-offs inherent in the subsequent decisions of other value-chain participants, as we saw with Blockbuster. VHS tapes that movie studios priced at $65 apiece meant that Blockbuster would order far fewer tapes than was optimal for its business model. Likewise, when an aggressive first-mover innovation changes the game in a particular industry, the strength of the innovator's advantage derives partly from the degree to which followers are deprived of flexibility in deciding how to respond.

The key to changing the *when* of the business model is to identify the organization's key decisions and understand when information adequate to make them becomes available at acceptably low risk. More often than not, however, organizations make key decisions without adequate information in hand. This problem accounts for inefficiencies that are apparent everywhere, revealing the low-information bets so many businesses make on products that badly miss the market—unread books, unsold computers, unwanted garments, unseen movies, unsold cars. Thus, any organization that can move decision making closer to the availability of better information stands to profit handsomely. Likewise, you may find it equally rewarding (or a necessary complement) to reshuffle the decision pattern by changing the order in which decisions are made; often some combination of closing the information gap and changing the decision sequence will produce the optimal business model innovation.

We have identified three different approaches you might use, depending on the circumstances, to innovate the *when* aspect of key business model decisions. We look first at changing the *timing of decisions* to postpone them to as late in the process as possible (or, in the most radical cases, until *whenever*). Next we show how you might *change the sequence of decisions* while leaving the time frame intact. For instance, some firms don't have the option of changing the time frame by which they operate, but they can shuffle the decision-making order so as to delay investment commitments—and mitigate risk—until pertinent information is known. Our third strategy involves *splitting decisions into stages* in order to obtain increasingly refined information before the decision is finalized.

Delaying Decisions to Gain Maximum Flexibility

As we saw earlier in the case of Zara, the fast-fashion model shifts the design and assortment decision to a later point in the cycle. Another manifestation of the same idea is the widely used strategy of production postponement.[1] Benetton, Hewlett-Packard, and Campbell Soup have all employed this approach. Using postponement strategy in your business model delays product-differentiation decisions until the last possible moment. Benetton originally innovated its business model to address information inefficiencies in the production of sweaters. The traditional process involves first dyeing the yarn, then knitting it into sweaters, and subsequently selling them through the retail network. The knitting process typically takes as long as sixty days to complete. Benetton improved its business model simply by postponing the dyeing process.

In the new approach, Benetton first knitted undyed yarn into different sweater styles (see figure 4-1). Crucially, however, it delayed dyeing the garments in different colors. This gave it an extra sixty days or more in which to gather market intelligence that could improve its bets on which colors would likely sell best. By changing the *when* of its key differentiation (color) decisions, Benetton was able to improve the business model so as to reduce associated information inefficiencies.

Time affects all areas of business operation. For example, price setting is among the most important decisions in many companies' business models. But making pricing decisions far ahead of the selling season increases the likelihood that prices will be set inefficiently—either too low

FIGURE 4-1

Postponement at Benetton

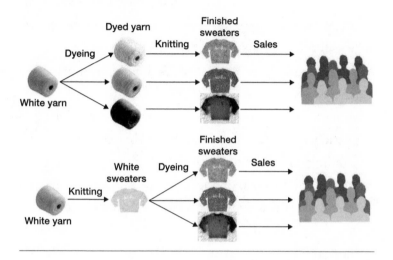

or too high. An alternative to becoming time's hostage in setting prices is to make it your ultimate ally by building a model that allows price to be flexibly adaptable to new information.

Airlines were among the first US industries to devise a BMI solution to this challenge. Once the airlines were deregulated, in 1978, they were free to set whatever prices they wanted. This soon led to the emergence of *dynamic pricing* as a powerful tool to deal with information inefficiency. Predicting demand for airplane seats is especially difficult because demand on any given route is highly contingent on economic conditions and can vary by the time of the day, day of the week, or week of the month. An airplane seat is a perishable commodity; empty seats on a plane today have no value whatsoever tomorrow. Airline capacity and staffing levels, on the other hand, are relatively fixed. High variability plus high fixed costs are a bad combination, increasing the likelihood of information inefficiencies.

American Airlines is credited with having pioneered the practice whereby prices could be changed at any time depending on updated information about customer demand. It might be more accurate to say that American invented an IT system—known as Sabre—that made it relatively easy to change prices quickly by factoring in new information. (American spun off Sabre in 2000. Among its offerings is a service that helps client firms set prices more efficiently.) Though every airline now has something comparable to Sabre, at the time it was one of the earliest examples of using IT to capture a sustainable competitive advantage. Suppose, for example, that on a Sunday, the Toronto Blue Jays beat the Baltimore Orioles to clinch a spot in the World Series, and need to travel to St. Louis on Wednesday for the opening game against the Cardinals. Suddenly, Toronto fans are scrambling for tickets to St. Louis. Fares rise sharply between the two cities (or to either city from other US airports), and fall for flights to Baltimore. This is dynamic pricing in action.

The ability to price dynamically changed the airline industry forever, allowing airlines to revise earlier pricing decisions on the fly, as better information became available. American Airlines was well positioned to innovate through Sabre (which originally stood for Semi-Automated Business Research Environment) because it had pioneered a pre-internet global reservation system (for use by travel agents) that compiled a large database of information on worldwide flights, reservations, and passengers. This was the germ of what ultimately began the *when*-driven transformation of the airline industry. Prices no longer had to be set only once, well in advance; they could be set and reset as often as needed to reflect real-time demand fluctuations. That is why, on any given flight, there are tremendous variations from passenger to passenger—even within the same seating class—in the price each has actually paid to fly.

More and more industries have come to realize that setting prices once and never changing them results in huge information inefficiencies. Internet retailers now change prices daily, often hourly, and multiple websites—including Pricespider.com, CamelCamelCamel.com, Nextag. com, and Decide.com—aggregate and use this information to help buyers find the best bargains among retailers' increasingly complex pricing schemes.[2] Online retailers are not alone in their ability to combat information inefficiency by changing prices. Kohl's was among the first to equip its stores with digital price tags, which can be adjusted remotely in response to fluctuating demand.

It's even possible to go beyond broad demand trends. No matter how often you change prices, they still apply to all your customers. But what if you could delay quoting a price until you knew enough about the individual customer to make the best possible decision? The casino and hospitality company Caesars Entertainment (acquired by Harrah's Entertainment in 2005) uses a sophisticated database compiled through Caesars' Total Rewards loyalty program. When a repeat customer calls to make a reservation, the agent asks for his Total Rewards number, which links to detailed information about the customer's gambling habits (including average bet size) and hence the profit he is likely to bring to the casino.[3] Depending on the Total Rewards profile, the customer may hear anything from "Sorry, all rooms are booked" to "You're in luck! We are happy to offer you a complimentary stay in our Presidential Suite!" In this case, the booking and pricing decisions are entirely contingent on individual customer information. And Caesars, by setting aside premium rooms for its most profitable clients, dramatically increases its revenues.[4]

To an extent, this sort of big-data and analytics-driven real-time flexibility may seem unfair in the way it rewards some customers while penalizing others, but it is increasingly common in business models. Amazon and other online retailers have been known to vary prices based on an individual customer's historical price tolerance. The gambit is simply a more sophisticated variant of the deft negotiation tactics of salespeople in auto dealerships, as they size up car buyers and put them in crude buckets: hard bargainers, recreational hagglers, the cost-insensitive, and the overcommitted easy marks.

CAVEATS: Naturally, the ability to exploit a strategy of postponing decisions until information becomes available relies on the assumption that we learn important new information over time and that the organization is flexible enough to act on it. In the case of Benetton, postponement reduces information risk, but it may also increase supply chain complexity. For airlines and gaming casinos, flexibility is achieved through significant investments over time in sophisticated IT systems that collect and analyze big data. Some businesses will conclude that the costs of flexibility trump the reduction in risk. Consequently, the BMI template of delaying decisions works best when the gains from better information are higher than the costs of creating flexibility in the system. In particular, this is likely to be the case where products are modular in nature and can be made relatively quickly, and when the uncertainty around market conditions is high.

Changing the Decision Sequence: Revolution through Competition

On October 4, 2004, SpaceShipOne rocketed into history, becoming the first private manned spacecraft to soar higher than 328,000 feet twice within a two-week period. No longer was space flight the exclusive province of government. A new private industry was born, and the project—led by aerospace designer Burt Rutan and software billionaire Paul Allen—won the $10 million Ansari X Prize, the bounty offered to the first nongovernment entity to complete two successful round trips into space within fourteen days.[5] (Creation of the X Prize was inspired by the $25,000 Orteig Prize, offered to the first person to fly nonstop from New York to Paris. It led, in 1927, to Charles Lindbergh's landmark transatlantic flight, an achievement that provided momentum for the worldwide development of commercial aviation.)

Most product development efforts begin with a proposed new technology for the development of which investments are raised. If, after initial investments, the technology proves to be a dud, then it's back to a drawing board. But the X Prize switched the order of decisions: would-be competitors first invested in developing the technologies required for nongovernment manned space flight. Only after the superior competitor proved its worthiness was the real investment made to further develop the winning approach.

Changing the decision-making sequence shifted the risks of development to the more than two dozen X Prize competitors, increasing the likelihood that a workable solution would emerge. A traditional top-down process would have involved soliciting proposals, evaluating their dry prose and the proponents' respective track records, and trying as best as possible to pick a winner from among the competing proposals' claims and technical approaches. A bottom-up effort, on the other hand, places no bets on a winning technology or team. Instead, it triggers a contest that delivers a proven winner before any serious money is committed; only the winning team is paid. The $10 million purse can be thought of as a relatively low entry price for a working prototype ready for commercialization (Paul Allen reportedly invested $25 million to develop SpaceShipOne).

This extraordinary reduction of risk is achieved simply by changing the sequence of decisions: from *investment first, performance after* to *performance first, investment after.* In the latter case, certainty replaces speculation, and the size of the prize is the carrot to persuade other parties to accept the burden of development risk.

More carrots are appearing in the open-innovation space. In the spirit of the X Prize, other types of incentive-based competition have become part of the corporate mainstream with the growth of open-innovation marketplaces created by such firms as InnoCentive and Hypios.[6] They offer rigorous approaches to helping their clients benefit from access to a global pool of innovative problem solvers from a range of disciplines. InnoCentive was launched in 2001 as a division of Eli Lilly and was spun out in 2005. Hypios is a European start-up launched in 2008 (one of the authors has advised the firm). Numerous other ventures have jumped into this space, including 99designs.

com, which serves graphic design needs, and Rentacoder. com and Topcoder, which run contests around software development challenges, and so on.

Open-innovation firms offer clients (seekers) a secure website on which to formulate and publish R&D problems to a global freelance community of qualified engineering, product-design, and scientific solvers. The firms help seekers define their problems with enough specificity to engage the interest of an appropriately skilled subset of solvers. Seekers offer monetary rewards for the right solutions (sometimes more than one may be selected), and solvers compete to develop the best solution and win the rewards. Problems might range from the chemical synthesis of a specific molecule to designing the look and feel of a new product.

To see why competitions are effective, consider how research-intensive firms typically operate. Most employ armies of experts to help them develop new technology or products. These experts have specialized knowledge and are often highly compensated. Each, in effect, is a specific type of asset with a very high fixed cost. Research is risky by its nature; the return from the work of your assembled experts is never easy to predict. Moreover, technological, environmental, and other types of disruptive change can force a firm to shift the focus of its R&D portfolio, suddenly rendering many of its experts' various specialties obsolete. The combination of high specialization, high cost, and a high rate of environmental flux makes the innovation function in many companies a huge source of information inefficiency yielding uncertain utility and returns.

Both Hypios and InnoCentive have hundreds of thousands of solvers within their freelance networks whose expertise is diverse enough that some will almost certainly possess skills that are relevant to any client's posted problem. It then falls to the client to evaluate solvers' solutions and select the most promising. While not all solvers necessarily deliver fully developed solutions, all are motivated to unambiguously demonstrate their solutions' feasibility and performance. The lever of certainty in this approach goes beyond the traditional response to a request for proposal (RFP). Seekers may not always get a satisfactory solution, but they will get a clear picture of each solver's capabilities. And the firms serve an intermediary role in helping seekers continuously clarify the problem and pushing solvers toward more-relevant solutions.

In almost all instances, contests (sometimes called "tournaments") are a more efficient mechanism for choosing among many risky options when it is hard to predict which would be most successful. The traditional sequence of events when solving any technological challenge is for the organization to: (1) select the most promising technology, design, or individual; (2) invest significant resources in developing the technology (or training the individual scientist, engineer, or designer); and (3) after what is often

FIGURE 4-2

Comparing decision sequences: traditional problem solving versus tournaments

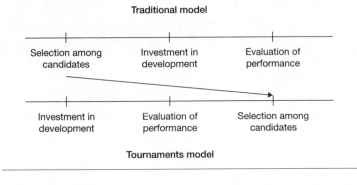

a long genesis, learn the results of its selection and investment when the new product's performance is revealed. As countless businesses can attest, innovations produced in this sequence often fail to perform as promised!

Figure 4-2 compares the traditional approach with the sequence of events in the tournament model: a seeker organization invites contestants to (1) solve a defined problem by developing technology, a design, or their own ideas; (2) demonstrate unambiguously the performance of their proffered innovations; and (3) wait while the organization judges the performance of the competing solutions and selects the one that best addresses the defined problem.

As with the X Prize, seeker firms commit no investment until the winning solution emerges. There are other benefits as well. They avoid the fixed costs of employing experts, instead paying only for output—the solution that best meets their research needs. This limits the risk of supporting an in-house capability that may not have a solution to the problem at hand. Even companies with a capable R&D function may want to use an innovation marketplace as a relatively low-risk way of expanding into less-familiar knowledge domains. And it is quite possible that the lure of the prize may motivate freelance experts to work just a bit harder than in-house talent, leading to more and better solutions for the firm. The freelance experts, on the other hand, bear the downside risk of investing their time in vain on a solution that is likelier to be rejected than chosen. However, if theirs is the chosen solution, they are likely to earn a substantial return on the invested time and effort.

The glaring inefficiency of the traditional model is its reliance on selecting the winning candidate solution long before any performance output becomes available. It is entirely possible that if one of the neglected candidates had been chosen instead, it would have delivered superior results. The high degree of selection uncertainty is the critical risk in the process. For instance, the performance of different space-travel technologies is highly uncertain, with any big bet on even one of the technologies carrying a significant risk—and space travel combines many new technologies. The tournaments model dramatically reduces the organization's risks and associated information inefficiencies.[7] (As you can see, in addition to changing the *when* aspect of the selection decision, the crowd-sourced tournament model has ancillary value as both a *who* and a *why* innovation: It transfers information risk to parties outside the company, and it modifies incentive structures to motivate those parties to work in your firm's interests.)

The tournament idea is quite versatile and can be applied to a variety of different domains, many of which are yet to be tested. Indeed, the universe of crowdsourcing and open-innovation approaches becomes increasingly attractive as industry ecosystems grow ever more volatile and uncertain. Tournaments are likely to substantially improve on business models that involve making bets on development with limited performance information. Likewise, the ability of organizations to respond quickly to fast-changing circumstances may require access to a much broader array of expert skills than any single business could easily or economically assemble. The more confounding the problem and the larger its scope, the more useful it will be to tap diverse and unexpected sources of insight or perspective. This is particularly true for the domains of scientific and medical research.

Changes to the sequence of business decisions can produce quite remarkable innovations in operational efficiency. Consider what you might suppose is a relatively stable and unexciting industry: the humble call center.

Shortly after Hurricane Katrina ravaged the Gulf Coast in August 2005, the American Red Cross called a start-up call-center company known as LiveOps with a challenging request: it needed to set up a large call center *within three hours* to help storm evacuees contact relatives. Several major outsourcers had already turned down the Red Cross request because they couldn't meet the tight deadline. But LiveOps was able to go live with four hundred agents in less than three hours. It handled more than seventeen thousand Katrina-related calls for the Red Cross, without requiring either LiveOps or the Red Cross to hire any new employees, invest in new facilities or equipment, or invest anything beyond limited managerial overhead.

Headquartered in Santa Clara, California, LiveOps is a private company with annual revenues of more than $200 million. Its chairman is former eBay chief operating officer and serial entrepreneur Maynard Webb. LiveOps has received around $51 million in venture funding from former eBay alumni and from Menlo Ventures, one of the largest technology-focused venture funds.[8] More than two hundred companies around the world, in a wide range of industries, use LiveOps' technology for multichannel interactions with customers.

Webb's background as a chief information officer may help explain why IT creatively pervades the LiveOps model. The firm uses a cloud-based networking and data platform studded with intelligent applications that stitch together and empower more than twenty thousand home-based independent customer-service agents. Whether you are ordering dinner from Pizza Hut or flowers from ProFlowers.com, you might be interacting with a Live-Ops call agent, possibly working from a cabin in Montana or a houseboat in Florida. (Agents working from home, using their own technology to access the LiveOps cloud platform, save the company the cost of developing and maintaining significant fixed infrastructure.) LiveOps handles both inbound customer inquiries and outbound sales operations.

The concept of LiveOps is to operate as a virtual call center and apply technology to address the business-model inefficiencies both of large physical call-center facilities and offshore operations.[9] LiveOps' home-based agents have full control of their schedules, giving them the latitude to work when they choose. This allows Live-Ops to recruit highly educated, highly motivated agents who prefer the unmatched flexibility of stay-at-home jobs (often they are people with child-care or other responsibilities). They become LiveOps virtual agents by passing an online test for each service they would like to handle. Agents indicate their availability to take calls by signing on to LiveOps' secure internet platform.

This is where the typical call-center decision pattern begins to get shuffled (see figure 4-3). Traditional outsourced call centers must make upfront investments in facilities

FIGURE 4-3

The LiveOps call-center model

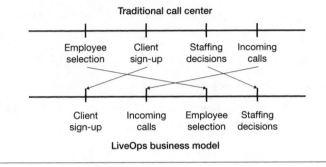

Traditional call center

Employee selection — Client sign-up — Staffing decisions — Incoming calls

Client sign-up — Incoming calls — Employee selection — Staffing decisions

LiveOps business model

and hard infrastructure (primarily communications) before they sign a single client or take their first inbound call. They must also decide how many agents to have at what levels of skill and expertise, and then hire and train them. These investments in hiring and training make it likely that firms are committed to retaining their agents for a lengthy period of time. Then, in the meantime, they must sign up clients whose needs match the capabilities they have assembled. Beyond these long-range employment and training decisions, firms must also develop daily and weekly staffing plans to ensure that enough agents with the right skills will be available to handle incoming calls.

LiveOps, on the other hand, maintains a virtual workforce of independent agents who are willing to trade some employment and income security in order to gain needed flexibility. They sign in only when they're available to work; in practice, this means that individual agents who signal their availability join a pool of talent waiting to be "hired" once a call comes in that matches their skills and experience. Agents are paid based on the duration of the call and—since calls are automatically recorded and scored—on their level of proficiency at meeting callers' needs. Over time, agents accumulate a performance history in responding to different types of calls. This allows for finer gradations, in differing contexts, by which to evaluate individual proficiency—skills and experience, strengths and limitations, speed and accuracy—and the process of matching callers with agents becomes increasingly precise.

Because intelligent software routes callers to the most qualified available agents based on the nature of the call, capacity and staffing levels are constantly adjusted in real time to meet actual demand. If there is a spike in a certain kind of inquiry, those calls can be routed efficiently to the agents best qualified to handle them. If overall volume is unexpectedly high or low, available agents are hired (or not) as needed, while in a traditional call center with a fixed shift size, many agents are either underutilized during slow periods or callers experience long wait times when the call volume spikes.

In figure 4-3, there are two focal decisions in the traditional call-center business model. The first is the employee selection (hiring) decision, which requires making bets on future employee performance and the level of customer demand for their skills. Second are the daily staffing decisions, which must set capacity sufficiently high to meet service-level guarantees. All of the agents staffed for a particular shift must be paid their wages, even though fewer than half, on average, are productively engaged at any given moment. Both of these decisions are risky bets that must be made in the face of high uncertainty. Because information inefficiency is high, bad bets occur frequently, leaving firms saddled with underperforming, underutilized employees whose skills don't match the market's demands.

As you can see, the LiveOps model changes the sequence of the two focal decisions. The hiring and daily staffing decisions are solved simultaneously, based on call volume and observed demand. Essentially, every time a call comes in, LiveOps makes the decision to hire an employee with the appropriate skill set and to staff her to handle that call. Consequently, as in the tournament model, LiveOps doesn't need to select *any* new employees in advance or make bets on their skill sets; nor must it try to predict fluctuations in day-to-day demand. Put differently, the LiveOps model changes the timing, or the *when,* prescribed for both decisions to the point of demand being realized. It operates a real-time employee hiring and staffing system just as Dell produces computers to order.

CAVEATS: There are limits to what you can achieve solely by changing the sequence of decisions. For instance, because LiveOps hires employees on demand, it is difficult to train them in advance to perform especially sophisticated tasks. Real-time hiring and staffing is best suited to such straightforward tasks as simple order taking. And since LiveOps agents take the risk of being idle and not making money, the business model depends on an ample supply of people for whom downtime has a relatively low cost. Further, there may be cases where the risk eliminated through resequencing does not justify the necessary costs, for example, when demand is very stable. In such cases, you may want to consider a different approach: splitting decisions into phases as more complete information becomes available.

Split Decisions to Gather Early Signs of Demand

A French internet retailer called MyFab engaged in an innovative experiment aimed at eliminating information risk in demand prediction. Its innovative business model invited customers to vote for their favorite furniture pieces from an online catalogue of potential designs. MyFab didn't manufacture anything until after the votes had been tallied; only the most popular items would be slated for production. Customers who voted for those popular designs were offered a 10 percent discount if they decided to buy.[10] The manufactured products were shipped to buyers directly from the factory, with no retail outlets, inventories, complicated distribution, or logistics networks.

What MyFab's BMI accomplished was to split its customers' buying decision into two parts. The first part was the decision to vote—from among many options—for a preferred selection of furniture items; the second was the decision to purchase one or more of the most popular items once they'd been manufactured. While the input MyFab gathered through the voting process was not a commitment in the form of an order, it was nonetheless a strong indication of customers' preferences. As such, it has value as a reasonable predictor of likely demand, amounting to a sort of half twist on Dell Computer's make-to-order innovation.

A group of Paris-based entrepreneurs launched MyFab in late 2008. Its products are quite similar—often identical—to those of its competitors, and the mainly Western markets it targets are already saturated with creative designers and efficient producers. So it needed a way to stand out. To do that, MyFab designed no new products and invented no breakthrough technology. All it did was change the traditional operating model of the industry. After its first three years of existence, MyFab's innovative business model helped it expand beyond France into new markets, including the United States.

MyFab, unlike most of its competitors, chose not to rely on forecasts of market trends to make selection and manufacturing decisions. Instead it created its catalog of possible designs, none of which were yet in production. In some cases, it hadn't even have arranged for the capabilities to produce them. (Why go to the trouble without a compelling reason?) It was simply unwilling to risk betting badly on customer tastes without first exploring ways of making surer bets—and why not trust the so-called "wisdom of crowds"?[11] So it waited for the customers to vote.

The engagement and social aspects of voting attracted customers in droves. But low prices kept them coming back. MyFab offered products at significantly lower prices than established furniture retailers. How? Because its business model was extremely efficient. The valuable information it gathered on furniture design trends gave it a better grip on both customer taste and likely demand. This reduced its exposure to stock-outs and excess inventory. That, in turn, increased top-line revenues and bottom-line profits. And being an online direct-to-consumer business, it needed no retail outlets of its own and no intermediary channel. Through lower prices, MyFab shared some of the benefits of these efficiencies with customers.

Like all the other examples described in this chapter, MyFab changed the timing of decisions prescribed by the traditional business model, thereby reducing its characteristic inefficiencies. Kickstarter, the popular crowd-funding website for creative projects, takes a different angle on decision splitting. Rather than merely ask users to vote for their preferences, it asks them to invest. Kickstarter facilitates projects by allowing project owners—musicians, filmmakers, photographers, painters, authors, some food entrepreneurs, product designers, and engineers—to solicit would-be customers' funding pledges for well-defined projects. Every proposed project has a funding goal (typically the seed money needed to get a project off the ground) and a deadline in which to raise it. If the specified goal is not achieved by the deadline, no funds are collected and the project does not go forward.

Founded in 2008 by Perry Chen, Yancey Strickler, and Charles Adler, Kickstarter has tapped into the enthusiasm of many devotees of artistic and entrepreneurial endeavors to support various kinds of creative projects. As of January 2014, there had been more than 130,000 launched projects (4,275 in progress), with a success rate of 44 percent—success being defined as achieving the targeted sum by the deadline. The successful projects had raised a total of $947 million.[12] Kickstarter itself reportedly raised $10 million in funding from backers including New York City–based venture firm

Union Square Ventures and angel investors such as Jack Dorsey, Zach Klein, and Caterina Fake.[13]

While Kickstarter and MyFab operate in very different industries and contexts, they share some key commonalities when compared with traditional models. Usual practice in developing a line of furniture for a conventional furniture designer or retailer is, first, for an in-house team to produce a great number of possible designs. Then an empowered group within the firm sorts through the options and places bets on the designs that seem most promising. The firm then arranges to source and produce, ship, and sell the selected designs. Finally, the finished products arrive on the retail floor. If the firm has bet on the right design options, then the chosen products become popular and the business model is validated. But if the selections are not popular, the firm is unlikely to recoup its investment in—much less profit from—having developed the line.

But the selection process at MyFab was designed to elicit far more reliable evidence. Instead of having a handful of executives guess what customers will want, My-Fab went straight to the customers and put the question to them directly: which of these furnishings would you be most likely to buy? This model raises the question of whether customers can be trusted to vote honestly. The "investment" they make in the voting process, motivated by the discount they will get if they ultimately make a

---

Good News and Bad News Are Both News

Failures should be studied. Apart from what MyFab learns from the votes its customers cast for their favorite furniture designs, the votes they don't cast are valuable, too. When customers go through MyFab's catalog of possibilities, they are shaping and refining the firm's understanding of taste. The same is true of creative artists who propose Kickstarter projects. Those that fail to raise the specified sum of seed money by their deadlines nonetheless prevent what might otherwise have been costly bad bets. Artists are learning very particular lessons that don't always bear precisely on their projects' artistic merit; what they are learning is what the market values. Over time, from project to project, they develop a surer sense of where artistic merit and commercial value intersect. Where are your business's most valuable learning opportunities?

---

purchase, creates an incentive for truthfulness.[14] In My-Fab's split-decision model, the most important decision is the prepurchase vote, because it is timed before the company makes consequential investments in developing the product. These early truthful signals on customer preference sharply reduce the risk of a bad investment. (See the sidebar, "Good News and Bad News Are Both News.")

Kickstarter provides a platform on which creative, enterprising individuals can test the potential market for their projects. Like MyFab, project proposers benefit from the same sort of customer voting system as the one MyFab operates. This is an improvement over traditional practice, whereby artists relied on their own insight, intuitions, and beliefs—or sought advice from a closed circle of friends and peers. Kickstarter allows them to audition projects (artists frequently propose a number of projects simultaneously), giving potential customers the opportunity, in effect, to prepurchase. Again, the change to the business model shifts part of the customer purchasing decision so that it precedes any substantial investment, reducing the risk of a bad bet (see figure 4-4).

Both the MyFab and Kickstarter models bring greater certainty to highly risky, unscientific processes. Splitting purchase decisions into a preliminary, feedback-producing phase followed by a purchase-commitment phase brings

FIGURE 4-4

The Kickstarter/MyFab business model

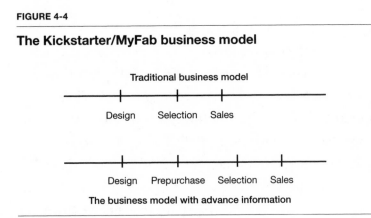

Traditional business model

Design   Selection   Sales

Design   Prepurchase   Selection   Sales

The business model with advance information

early actionable insight to a process that has more typically operated as a guessing game.

CAVEATS: Designing a successful decision-splitting strategy depends on finding decisions that can be divided so as to produce early information gain. In some cases, decision splitting cannot be done at all because the decision process is not divisible (you can't price a little bit now and a little bit later). In other cases, it can be done only at some additional cost, and risk-return calculations will need to be performed. You must also be careful to design the right incentive to induce customers to share information. Is compensation high enough to induce the customer to reveal true information, or is clicking a few buttons too time consuming relative to the benefit? These sorts of uncertainties invite experimentation—a topic we will cover in chapter 7.

Another relevant development is the lean start-up movement, which is taking the corporate innovation and start-up worlds with a storm. At the heart of the movement is a radical philosophy for changing the timing of key decisions for starting new ventures or developing new products in established companies. Traditionally, starting a risky new venture entailed putting together a detailed business plan that would cover all essential pieces of the business model and then executing the plan in a relatively insular fashion, stealth mode.

The lean start-up approach, on the other hand, recommends splitting up the key decisions on business model design into numerous sequential phases, interleaved with extensive testing, experimentation, and data collection from customers, partners, regulators, and so on. The venture starts with relatively imprecise and limited hypotheses on where an opportunity for a new venture may lie as opposed to a detailed business plan. This is followed by multiple stages of information gathering and "pivoting," or revising the business model to arrive at the final validated business model. What was once a single business model decision is split into many sequential decisions, each benefiting from information gathered between stages.

TAKEAWAYS

A few simple rules can help you innovate by changing the *when* of key business decisions:

Delay decisions as long as possible. If the opportune moment for obtaining information is fixed in time, you can attempt to postpone decisions as long as possible to bring them closer to that moment.

Change the sequence of decisions. Changing the decision-making sequence can be a way to incorporate more information into the process. Some companies have reduced their R&D risks in this way and others reduced inefficiencies in the way they produce products and services.

Split a key decision into phases so as to obtain early information, before the decision is completed. Even when decision sequence can't be changed, you may still be able to gather highly useful preliminary information before committing to a key decision. As MyFab and Kickstarter have shown, the right incentive can entice your customers to offer early indications of their relative enthusiasm for the various directions you might pursue.

When Innovation in Action:
The Supersonic Vending Machine

Products sold in a vending machine are a lot like fashion apparel; this season's peacock is next season's feather duster. Just like Zara, a vending machine that has the right product in stock at the right time can make a high margin sale: if it is raining, umbrellas fly off the shelves; if it is sunny, sunscreen and shades are most valuable (with markups of four to five times the cost). In both cases, the conventional business model is plagued with information risks, and decisions on assortment are made well before an apparel retailer knows the fashion trends and the vending machine provider knows the weather. What if we applied the technique of delaying decisions, which has so successfully transformed the apparel industry, to the vending machine industry and created a supersonic vending machine? The assortment of a traditional vending machine is decided once every six months (or even less often), and the machine is then supplied through a logistics system that values lower costs rather than speed of replenishment. In the supersonic vending machine concept (which a participant in one of our innovation workshops conceptualized), the assortment and stock quantity in a vending machine would be updated daily or more often. If rain is forecast, more shelf space would be dedicated to umbrellas; if it is going to be sunny, sunscreen, water, and shades are brought to the fore. The machines would be stocked and resupplied with daily visits by small urban vehicles (two-wheeled carts, urban tricycles, and so on). While this approach is more costly than traditional logistics, this technique would reduce information inefficiencies and increase sales, which would probably more than pay for the expenses.

In our ordering of the BMI levers, *when* is the second way to change the structure of decisions. It is also often the easiest one for organizations to play with. *When* can be changed within the organization and across the value chain. By brainstorming the time-sensitive consequences of all the possible decisions—as we describe in chapter 2—you will likely be able to identify multiple approaches to innovation.

Now we move on to a fundamentally different approach to eliminating inefficiencies. Rather than focusing on what decisions are made, and when, we focus next on who is the best choice to make key decisions.

CHAPTER 5

The *Who* Strategy

More than twenty-five years ago, Walmart and Procter & Gamble pioneered the transfer of decision rights governing the replenishment of store shelves.[1] Walmart surrendered those decisions to P&G because it saw that P&G was best positioned to optimize the entire value chain if Walmart gave it access to point-of-sale data. Armed with Walmart's demand information, P&G could optimize production and transportation logistics. Thus, what came to be known as vendor-managed inventory became the gold standard for many companies in the consumer packaged goods industry and beyond. It was a remarkable shift in the traditional business model. If a company as guarded about its information and decisions as Walmart could see the benefits of giving up those decision rights, surely other companies could summon the will to do likewise. And most of them did. Eventually.

To be sure, this transformative innovation required a lot of raw effort, IT capability, and investment, but it fundamentally changed supply chain management in the retail sector. At the heart of this BMI was Walmart's forward-thinking insight: suppliers possessed the right combination of information and incentives to keep Walmart well stocked with their products by optimizing delivery and production schedules. Why should Walmart continue doing what its partners could do better?

What Walmart recognized is this chapter's central insight: often a business model designates the wrong parties to make key decisions. As we have shown through many earlier examples, every such decision in your business model is subject to two classic types of risk: those that cause inefficiencies related either to a lack of necessary information or to misaligned incentives among parties who must collaborate to achieve a common goal. The likelihood of inefficiencies caused by either (or both) of these risks will increase or decrease depending on who makes these key decisions.

Some of these inefficiencies are the natural outcome of growth, as organizations have become global and more complex, with decisions now widely dispersed and key sources of input often inaccessible to the designated decision makers. Consequently, those currently empowered may no longer be in the best position to make the call. In this chapter, we will show you how to change your business models by selecting the best available decision maker. We will also explain how firms that innovate their business models by switching to superior deciders can achieve dramatically improved performance. (For other considerations, see the sidebar, "Make Culture Your Ally.")

We offer three BMI strategies for changing the *who*. First, we show how you can change your business model to *empower a better-informed decision maker*. In some cases, managers will delegate decisions to their better-informed employees; in other cases, an enterprise will delegate decisions to one or more channel partners. However, such people (or groups) may not exist because *all* of the possible deciders are equally ill informed. For those cases, we show how you can still innovate the business model by *selecting the decision maker who suffers the lowest consequences*—someone for whom the decision-related risks are closest to being negligible. Finally, we show how you can reduce risks by *selecting a decision maker who stands to benefit the most from the decision*. Typically, a decision maker who bears the brunt of a decision's economic consequences is likeliest to focus first and foremost on increasing the value to be created by the system.

When Information Is Power, Select the Best-Informed Decision Maker

A small revolution in the reallocation of decision-making authority has slowly spread across a number of industries, using strategies consisting of both direct employee empowerment and the delegation of formerly centralized choices to local authorities with better knowledge of customer needs and preferences. Increasingly, business models freely shift decisions to people whose knowledge of the marketplace or of their own performance capabilities puts them in the best position to make the call.

Make Culture Your Ally

How many organizations would have been as daring as Walmart in transforming inventory management? How many would have been as willing as Amazon to reconsider a foundational strategy like stockless fulfillment? And who but Google would, in effect, let highly paid engineers do their own thing for the equivalent of a day a week? *Who* innovations often transfer decisions rights, authority, responsibilities, and discretion from one part of the organization. For these delicate role reversals to be successful, it is imperative that the people involved are marshaled by a greater corporate mission rather than individual survival. In this regard, your corporate culture can be either an enabler or a brick wall. A culture that is built around a larger organizational mission (reducing prices, improving products, metrics, and so on) can help the individuals concerned see the larger organizational gains rather than fixate on their changed roles. In approaching any *who* innovation effort, try to make your culture your ally rather than your opponent.

The innovation Walmart pioneered with P&G was all about delegating decisions to the best-informed party. We described Zara's fast-fashion business model in chapter 2. Though Zara's was predominantly a *when* innovation, one key aspect of its strategy hinged on a *who* innovation. Instead of having design and assortment decisions made centrally by senior executives, Zara empowers local store managers to share in the decision making and add input about the fashion designs that local customers want most. That, of course, means that Zara must consequently manage more supply chain complexity, owing to potentially greater assortment variation from store to store. But the success of the fast-fashion model depends on always having the best available information; the ability to act on local insights offers a compelling trade-off.

Both the Walmart and Zara examples depend on a level of trust (between Walmart and its strategic suppliers and between Zara's executives and its local store managers). Google, too, has developed a trust-based management innovation. Typically, the managers of a business set their employees' agendas and the way they allocate their time. However, Google has changed the *who* of this traditional management function by giving employees greater latitude to choose their own paths. Technical staffers are asked to spend 20 percent of their time on projects of their own devising. (Even letting one's mind wander counts toward that quota.) In a company that aspires to continuous invention, it is a legitimate BMI to free people to allocate time to their own ideas. The allocation of specific budgeted time gives credence to Google's creative culture and lets the best-informed decision maker, the employee herself, choose whatever challenge she is most passionate and capable of tackling. It also circumvents the tendency of managers to form judgments about ideas before they've been adequately developed, refined, and tested.

People aren't merely daydreaming. Empowering smart individuals to set their own course for a portion of the workweek pays important dividends. According to an April 2008 *Harvard Business Review* article, in one six-month period, Google engineers' 20 percent projects led to fifty new Google offerings "accounting for half of all new products and features (including Gmail, AdSense, and Google News)" developed during that time.[2]

Groups of *Who*s

There are situations when the *who* isn't a single individual. In some service-sector businesses, managers have delegated decisions about staffing and scheduling to a group of employees. Formerly, managers made these decisions, sometimes aided by workforce-management systems that forecast labor demand based on historical data. In the restaurant business, for example, these systems proved to be very blunt instruments. They often resulted in servers being scheduled for shifts they would rather not work and not scheduled for those they preferred. Worse, they often slotted less-productive servers for shifts that offered the richest up-selling opportunities, while high performers got stuck with less-promising shifts.

The Boston-based restaurant chain, Not Your Average Joe's, is trying to make smarter resource-allocation decisions. In an industry where productivity standards haven't changed in many years, Not Your Average Joe's is looking for innovative ways to match the best talent to the richest revenue opportunities. Using an analytic tool called Muse, which tracks servers' performance over time in terms of sales per customer (as measured by check size) and customer satisfaction (as measured directly or by tips), the chain has developed a productivity-based ranking system whereby servers get to schedule themselves, choosing—in order of rank—both their shifts and the sections of tables they want to serve.[3]

Of course, servers don't have absolute freedom. The system ensures that even decisions delegated to employees are governed by the productivity measures most relevant to the restaurant's performance. In that sense, the ranking system serves as a safety net for the firm's interests. And since top-ranked servers typically choose the best shifts and tables, it also motivates lower-productivity servers to improve their performance and thus move up in the pecking order—or else change careers.

Not Your Average Joe's has much to gain by delegating slotting and staffing decisions to servers. Data shows that the most productive server brings in $10 more per check than the group average, whereas the least productive server brings in $20 less. On the busiest shifts and at the best tables, there's a lot of revenue at stake. An empowered, performance-ranked system of resource allocation maximizes opportunities and minimizes liabilities.

Another group-focused *who* innovation is the delegation of decisions about what new features and capabilities to include in future products and services to customers. Eric von Hippel, a professor of technology innovation at MIT's Sloan School of Management, has spent years developing the idea that "active customers" are prolific sources of innovation. Von Hippel explored the role the "lead users" of high-tech companies' software played in proposing ideas for future improvements. More recently, he surveyed the variety and extent of consumer innovations in the United States, the United Kingdom, and Japan.[4] If a business can tap into customer thinking, it can extend its innovative reach and encounter entirely unexpected ideas.

Naturally, you must be careful not to transfer decision-making power to a party that is perfectly informed but

CAVEATS: While the advantages of making decisions using better information are obvious, employee or partner empowerment and extensive data collection come with costs and difficulties. In the case of Walmart, for example, there was a considerable upfront investment in technology. Further, there was also the need to negotiate and coordinate complicated new relationships with trading partners, which included changing the way their supply chains operated and facilitating their access to Walmart's internal systems. Moreover, as Not Your Average Joe's may discover, it can be a leap of faith to surrender some degree of management control to technology. And if you lack the creative mission of a Google, you may be unwilling to allow employees the freedom to pursue agendas you are not setting. Finally, perhaps your workforce—unlike that of a restaurant—isn't scheduled or compensated in ways that would take full advantage of a rankings-based empowerment system.

inefficiently aligned with respect to incentives. In the cases of Zara and Walmart, incentives are well aligned. With Not Your Average Joe's, you can argue that its software program is free of incentive-alignment issues; all it does is analyze objective performance data in order to produce a ranking that allocates the best (most revenue-optimizing) choices to the top performers. But that may not always be the case. The benefits of a well-informed decider are wasted if misaligned incentives undercut the value of better information. As we explore in the next section, in situations where everyone is equally ill informed, it is preferable to transfer decision making to the party *best able to manage or bear the risk.*

The Lesson of Internet Retail:
Discover Who Bears the Least Consequences

You might suppose—incorrectly—that Amazon.com was the world's first internet bookseller. Book Stacks Unlimited came first, back in 1992, whereas Amazon didn't ship its first book until 1995. Nevertheless, it soon managed to dominate the online book market and eventually the wider e-commerce domain. It did so while consistently staying in the top ranks of customer satisfaction and service quality.[5]

Amazon grew from zero revenues in 1995 to $61 billion in 2012, making CEO and founder Jeff Bezos one of the innovative titans of the internet age. Although many of Amazon's innovations were plainly technological, the key to its early prosperity was a business model that changed the *who* for a number of the company's key decisions.

From the very beginning, Amazon's operation was organized around a "sell all, carry few" business model. When Bezos stated, in Amazon's first annual report, "Our store would now occupy six football fields," the operative word was "would," since it hinted at Amazon's ambitious virtuality. At the time, the company's only warehouse, in Seattle, could have occupied scarcely one football field. Yet, even in 1995, Amazon offered more than a million books, while stocking relatively few—roughly two thousand of the most popular titles. Most other titles were sourced through "drop-shipping" arrangements. Amazon simply forwarded customer orders to book wholesalers or publishers, which then shipped the products directly to consumers using Amazon's packaging materials and labels.

This stockless business model allowed Amazon to offer many more books than any physical retailer without carrying them as inventory. Big inventories of books—including many titles with low or unpredictable demand—require both large cash investments and warehouse space. At its founding, Amazon had neither; it was then far smaller than most of the publishers with which it did business. Every back-catalog book it ordered would have come with the risk of demand never materializing. Traditional retailers like Barnes & Noble, the giant of bricks-and-mortar bookselling, managed this dilemma by limiting customer choice; they stocked only relatively popular titles. It was simply too inefficient for bricks-and-mortar firms to stock books with spotty, risk-riddled demand.

Amazon's solution was to change who made stocking decisions and thereby transfer the risk of being stuck with inventory to the parties best able to bear them. In the stockless model, Amazon's network of book wholesalers and publishers each independently managed their assortments and inventories. They, not Amazon, bore the consequences of information risk. But because the risk was widely distributed, the many individual wholesalers and publishers were able to manage it with relative ease. Had Amazon not done this, the cumulative risk it would have borne would have been financially intolerable for any company, let alone an internet start-up. The strategy of delegating all of the decision making and the associated information risk across a network of virtual partnerships ensured Amazon's early success.

Today those innovations are well-recognized advantages that online retailers routinely enjoy. Amazon extended the lessons of its early BMI experiments into many nonbook product categories. The drop-shipping model has even spawned an internet service intermediary called DropShip Commerce, which is building a platform to seamlessly connect thousands of retailers with thousands of wholesalers, to arrange drop-shipment for any kind of product.[6]

Not every business model absorbed Amazon's bookselling lessons. Barnes & Noble couldn't shake free of its bricks-and-mortar history. While it carried more titles online than it did in its stores, it decided against a drop-ship strategy, making the curious decision to carry all of the books it offered on its website in inventory. Internet sales for Barnes & Noble have been static for many years, while Amazon has kept growing. (For more about Amazon, see the sidebar, "How Amazon Keeps Changing the *Who* of Its Business Model.")

Of course, the Amazon model doesn't work for everyone. We have studied dozens of internet retailers—both successful and bankrupt—and it is clear that drop-shipping arrangements are difficult to manage and were largely responsible for a number of bankruptcies in the early internet era.[7]

Among the most prominent failures was ValueAmerica .com, a web portal where customers could find a broadly diverse assortment of products. Like Amazon and others, ValueAmerica.com acted as an order-taking hub, delegating picking, packing, and shipping to its partner manufacturers—each one a node in a very large network. Founded in 1996, the start-up styled itself as virtual Walmart. But it failed to master the disciplined management oversight and communication needed to keep a drop-shipping network humming efficiently. Thus, there was a wide gap between the costs of coordinating a large corps of manufacturers, whose logistic and execution capabilities varied widely, and the benefits of reducing information risk. Uneven fulfillment performance led to

How Amazon Keeps Changing the *Who* of Its Business Model

What has made Amazon a truly great company is its constant reevaluation of its business model; it pivots from one model to another as circumstances warrant. What started as a decision to change the *who* of key assortment and inventory decisions in its business model—delegating to publishers and distributors—has gradually transformed over time into a more traditional retail model. For instance, Amazon has steadily increased the number of titles it stocks internally. There are many reasons for this:

- As the scale of Amazon's operations grew, its catchment area became larger than that of many publishers. The risk situation reversed, with Amazon now enjoying *lower* information risk than those to whom it had earlier delegated selection decisions.

- Further, with the benefit of historical information and extensive data-analysis capabilities, Amazon was able to more accurately estimate the demand for many books than were their publishers.

- Finally, the fulfillment efficiency of Amazon eventually eclipsed that of any of its channel partners; nor did any partner have the scale to handle Amazon's sales volume.

Moreover, as e-commerce has matured, it is now harder to dominate the online retail space based on product selection alone. Although Amazon was still beating bricks-and-mortar retailers in breadth of selection—in many categories, not just books—other internet retailers adopted variants of drop-shipping and were able to offer similarly wide and deep stock-less product availability. Once that happened, Amazon again pivoted its business model to compete on *quality* of fulfillment and capitalize more on economies of scale and data expertise than on its vast assortment.

All of these advances led to a reversal of the "sell all, carry few" business model; now it has morphed into "sell all, carry more." And, in 2006, Amazon unveiled a program called Fulfillment by Amazon, whereby independent sellers could use Amazon's warehouse network to fill orders and delegate to Amazon their logistics-related decisions. Clearly, Amazon had come to see greater potential business value in transferring decision making back to itself.

Under this changed model, Amazon became a wholesaler of goods sold by many much smaller virtual storefronts. As in its initial drop-shipping model, the bigger firm with the larger catchment area is in a better position to bear the information risk. What the distributors and publishers, in the aggregate, were to Amazon in its early days, Amazon now can be to participants in its fulfillment-for-hire program. Most recently, Amazon unveiled yet another step in developing its own fulfillment capabilities: it is going to spend close to $14 billion to build about fifty new warehousing facilities to be able to reach most of the US population within the same day. For Amazon, the internet retail model has come full circle.

customer dissatisfaction. After a promising IPO in 1999, ValueAmerica went bankrupt the following year.

CAVEATS: Shifting information risk to the party best able to bear it is often an attractive strategy for overcoming information inefficiencies when there is clearly no decision maker who possesses superior information. However, there is at least one possible pitfall. Though a party might be well positioned to deal with the decision's consequences, its incentives may be misaligned with the interests of the value chain. In that case, delegating the decision could do more harm than good if, for example, you disclosed information that would allow a drop-shipper to poach your customers. Instead, you would be better off looking to the party with the most to gain.

Who Has the Greatest Stake in a Successful Outcome?

Sometimes the human needs a product addresses are so urgent and clear that it is impossible to imagine the product could fail. But even the most compelling benefits cannot overcome a fatal flaw in the business model.

Irrigation is one of the world's oldest commercial activities. It dates back to ancient Mesopotamia and Egypt, when the world population was miniscule. In the past fifty years, however, world population has doubled, and water for irrigation is a critical constraint in many countries, including Afghanistan.[8] Afghan farmers have long used drip irrigation, which drips water slowly to the roots of plants rather than spraying it in intense but less-targeted periodic bursts.[9] Drip irrigation (also called micro-irrigation) is regarded as a breakthrough agricultural innovation: It dramatically increases crop yields while reducing water consumption.

The technology behind drip irrigation is relatively simple and accessible (at least in the West), and the need for micro-irrigation strategies is widespread. There are a number of undifferentiated players in the industry, but an Israeli company called Netafim has managed to capture more than one-third of the micro-irrigation equipment market.[10] In the past fifteen years, Netafim's revenues have grown sixfold in an otherwise commoditized sector.

To be sure, Netafim, like other industry players, invested in R&D to improve its technology. But even its most innovative products didn't initially succeed as expected. In the 1990s, the firm introduced modern electronic control technology that included sophisticated sensor arrays. The sensors helped fine-tune water application based on the soil's water content, salinity, and fertilization, and on meteorological data. Netafim demonstrated that its system could increase crop yields by 300 to 500 percent, making it a potentially lucrative investment. Yet, it struggled to catch on.

Worse, it wasn't catching on with the very people who needed it most. In Central and South Asia—especially

Afghanistan and Pakistan—large sections of a fast-growing population make their living on subsistence agriculture.[11] With underdeveloped canal systems and no public or private investment in irrigation infrastructure, the vast majority of farmers rely on increasingly scarce rain and natural runoff. This scarcity makes these regions among the world's most underdeveloped and unstable. Yet, study after study has shown that improved irrigation systems could catalyze new development with the potential to transform life in these regions, bringing relief from a vicious cycle of poverty, insecurity, and underdevelopment.[12]

Though Netafim believed that its drip-irrigation system would have a huge social and economic impact, the company's efforts to refine the technology, grow awareness, and get support from regional power players—government, warlords, and insurgents—made little difference. When all else failed, Netafim began to consider a new culprit: the system's business model.

As it stood, Netafim's business model caused challenging information and incentive-alignment inefficiencies:

- **It required a customer leap of faith.** Farmers had to buy into the system with an irreversible investment. They recognized that investment as a certainty, but saw the proffered benefits as purely speculative.

- **It provoked incentive-based mistrust.** Farmers had no idea of the system's true performance. The company's

ROI calculations estimated the system's payback period at less than a year, but farmers were unconvinced. Netafim was clearly motivated to sell farmers drip-irrigation systems, so the farmers perceived that it had an incentive to make exaggerated performance claims.

- **It included unfamiliar new technology.** The sensor technology the systems incorporated was newfangled and unfamiliar. Although local farmers were expert at using traditional systems, they knew little about this high-tech approach. What could the sensors do that was worth the extra investment?

- **It was being applied in a problematic environment.** From Netafim's perspective, the region presented logistic challenges to deploying and maintaining systems. Rural areas had extremely poor roads and other infrastructure. (Netafim planned to use camels as its official corporate vehicle.) Many areas also featured unstable security conditions, and some people within the company questioned the wisdom of marketing the system in countries like Afghanistan.

An extra burden of information and incentive-alignment risks almost always stands in the way of new-technology adoption. Prospective customers perceive the risk and fear that it will fall on them should they be unwise enough to become early adopters. Businesses like Netafim must therefore find ways of reducing the perceived burden.

In its unproductive standoff with the very customers who would benefit most from its product, Netafim would have to reduce information and incentive-alignment inefficiencies by shifting the adoption decision to the party with the most to gain—itself. Only after that shift occurred would farmers be willing to say yes to Netafim.

To create new incentives that would favor adoption, Netafim put its money where its mouth was. It changed its revenue model by launching a new service-oriented offering that it called the "IrriWise Crop-Management System." IrriWise was an integrated package that included system design and installation, all required hardware, and periodic maintenance. Farmers didn't have to *buy* the system; it would be installed at Netafim's expense. Netafim's compensation would be earned over time, with revenues to be tied directly to each farmer's increased crop yields. Instead of selling systems and moving on to the next customer, Netafim was now incented to help farmers achieve the best possible outcome. The company even rewrote its mission statement from "making the best drip-irrigation equipment for customers" to "helping the world grow more with less"—a change that was much more than semantic.

Netafim had aligned its incentives with those of its customers. This allowed it to dramatically grow revenues and increase market share, while making a life-changing impact on some of the world's most impoverished citizens. These business benefits were possible because the end product of its new business model—achieved by recalibrating risks and incentives—was actually a higher level of customer comfort, belief, and trust. Instead of adopting a new technology, farmers adopted a service-based partnership. The key to this innovation was to change the *who* of the focal decision: how new technology was adopted. Netafim chose to absorb the risks of adoption because it was the party with the most to gain.

Even though farmers might still question Netafim's intentions and not fully believe its claims about system benefits, that no longer mattered; their outlook on adopting the technology was fundamentally changed because they could adopt it free from its greatest risks. The cost to farmers would be next to nothing unless the system actually worked, and even then only in proportion to the extent that it increased their crop yields. Netafim, on the other hand, not only bore the cost of the system; it also shared fully in the risks of poor crop yield caused by events beyond its control. It would share in the randomness of rain, sunshine, soil quality, equipment malfunction, and other vicissitudes that formerly affected only the farmers.

Why would Netafim willingly absorb these added information risks? Because, given its micro-irrigation expertise and its access to sophisticated forecasting technologies, the risks were a lot smaller for Netafim than for the farmers. Moreover, its size and diverse market base allowed it to spread the risk out, making the consequences far lower for Netafim than for an individual farmer. Even if the system were to fail in one region, Netafim could make up for it in other regions. As farmers achieved greater success, word would spread; Netafim would increase its sales and realize economies of scale that could improve the risk-return calculus of the farmers.

In slow- or no-adoption situations like this, buyers will always resist spending real money today for unproven benefits that only accrue later, if at all. In such circumstances, a *who* innovation can break the logjam. Economists have studied this phenomenon since the seventeenth century, using the term *moral hazard* to describe the effect of inefficiencies that occur when risks are displaced.[13] Nobel Prize–winning economist Paul Krugman once defined moral hazard as "any situation in which one person makes the decision about how much risk to take, while someone else bears the cost if things go badly."[14] Moral hazard has been at the root of numerous business model failures, most catastrophically the recent mortgage crisis.

Another example rich with moral hazard comes from the energy-efficiency industry. We are accustomed to thinking that green technologies come with a premium cost, much like the idea that organic foods cost more than their conventional counterparts. Such perceptions notwithstanding, just about any organization (or household) can become more sustainable and save money in the bargain. That's because energy efficiency has an enormous upside.

Many older homes and office buildings were designed without a conscience about consumption; and many older heating and lighting technologies have been replaced by more efficient alternatives. Replacement windows, more and better insulation, compact fluorescent lightbulbs, motion-activated light switches, and more efficient electric motors and heating technology all shrink the carbon footprint while lowering the overall cost of energy by driving down demand. In fact, energy-efficiency projects are the easiest and the fastest way to reduce greenhouse emissions, their return on invested capital is positive, and they can be done without new or unproven technology.[15]

Yet, the industry that has developed around various energy-efficiency solutions has so far struggled to successfully make its case to the market. Only a miniscule proportion of homes and businesses have implemented energy-efficiency projects. This looks like a Netafim-style paradox: customers who would benefit enormously are not embracing a simple solution to one of the world's most vexing problems.

In the commercial sector at least, the paradox has led to a Netafim-style business model innovation. Energy services companies (ESCOs) are firms that offer a variety of energy services: some are utilities; others manufacture control technology (devices and software), heating and cooling systems, or lighting equipment; and some are private- or public-sector energy-efficiency consultants.[16] Together, they shift the adoption risk associated with energy-saving technologies from their business customers onto themselves.

An ESCO begins by doing an energy audit of the customer's premises (using the customer's current utility costs as a reference point). The ESCO then implements whatever efficiency projects it decides are necessary (bearing all of the upfront costs itself). In subsequent years, all of the savings that result from these improvements are shared between the ESCO and the customer. Or, in some cases, for a contracted period of years, the customer pays an annual fee to cover the cost of the installed equipment and its maintenance (often with a guarantee that the fee will never exceed the realized savings).

Because the customer makes no upfront investment, it benefits from greatly reduced information risk (the uncertainty of the investment's outcome) while also realizing energy savings from higher efficiency. The ESCO benefits from its share of the customer's savings. Like Netafim, because it thoroughly understands the technology and can predict its performance, the ESCO bears the additional risk quite easily. Of course, for the customer, risk reduction comes at a price: by contract, it must share the long-term benefits with the ESCO, which will likely earn a healthy profit in exchange for assuming more risk. Over time, awareness of the benefits grows and resistance to adoption declines, resulting in accelerating market development. Consequently, the ESCO is the party with the most to gain. Businesses that don't like the ESCO terms can either stick with the status quo or shoulder the efficiency investments on its own. But ESCOs' *who* innovation has begun to get traction. The relatively young industry has grown at a rate of roughly 7 percent to 8 percent per year, even during the economic crisis.[17]

CAVEATS: Taking on more risk works for a company only if its relevant technology is reliable. Businesses like Netafim and the ESCO companies must take care not to go too far in taking on risk traditionally borne by customers. That possibility may be more likely in the ESCO example, since each customer an ESCO serves may present unique circumstances that dictate a custom (rather than a template) solution; in each such case, there is some chance of assuming more risk than necessary or miscalculating the incentives. For example, the savings from energy-efficient equipment may diminish if clients decide they can economically leave their lights on longer, once improvements have been implemented. Taken to an extreme, this is known as Jevons paradox: as technology makes consumption of a resource more efficient, it will lead to an increase in consumption of the resource—in this case, electricity.[18] To align incentives around objectives of both energy efficiency *and* conservation, the ESCO may need to resort to a *why* innovation: it can influence customer behavior by applying close monitoring and stringent contract terms.[19]

TAKEAWAYS

As organizations continue growing in complexity and global reach, decisions in them spread out, creating situations in which the historical decision maker may no longer be best suited to the role. In order to design innovative business models, changing who makes the decision can be an effective—even breakthrough—strategy. Three principles guide this innovation approach:

Transfer decision rights to the best-informed decision maker. When a better-informed decision maker is available, changing the *who* will lead to decisions that impose fewer information and incentive-alignment inefficiencies.

Transfer decision making to the party best able to tolerate the decision's consequences. When all possible deciders possess equally good (or imperfect) information, or when the motivation of the best-informed party is not aligned with the company, shifting a decision to the party who can best tolerate its risks can create value.

Move the consequences (costs) of the decision to the party that benefits the most. It is hard for customers to invest in a complicated product based on new technology; they mistrust the seller's benefit and performance claims.

In such cases, a firm should consider bearing the adoption risk. Because a firm has the most to gain if a market develops for its products, it is in its interest to bear the added risk, which it can tolerate more easily, being the best-informed party. (Least-informed parties almost always make suboptimal decisions because the consequences of a wrong decision could prove catastrophic.)

Who Innovation in Action: Where Is My FashionSista?

The greatest threats to the sartorial happiness of teenagers today are not the excesses of Miley Cyrus or Justin Bieber, but another, younger entity—Facebook. Ask any sartorially inclined teenager and he or she will tell you that the usable life span of an outfit has declined dramatically because of, you guessed it, Facebook. While in the good old days, an outfit could be safely worn on multiple occasions with disjoint attendees (say, a family outing, and an outing with friends), an outfit worn today is viewed by all attendees to the individual's virtual life that plays out 24/7 in the enduring annals of Facebook. But what if the teenager could be paired with another teenager who shares her size and fashion tastes? Or even better, not with just another teenager, but perhaps with a group of teenagers. By exchanging outfits, she could extend the usable life of outfits dramatically, while still providing the necessary fresh look for a new post on Facebook. But how to find such a group? Easy! Transfer these decisions to the best-informed decision maker.

This is exactly what FashionSista, a start-up that was born in one of our programs on innovation, attempted to do. Instead of teenagers or their parents trying to find partners for outfit swaps, FashionSista would build a database containing extensive information on what goes on in individual teenagers' closets. Based on this database, FashionSista would be able to accurately identify the individual fashion profile. Using this information, FashionSista would find an endless supply of other compatible teenagers to exchange outfits with. Transferring matching decisions from individuals to a market maker like FashionSista would eliminate the information inefficiency, keep outfits fresh, and eliminate many existential sartorial crises.

By now you understand what decisions to make, when to make them, and who should make them. You also have learned which parties are best equipped to bear the consequences of those decisions. The final dimension is to align the incentives that provide motivation for achieving the objectives at the root of those decisions—the *why* aspect of the decision pattern. That is the subject of the next chapter.

CHAPTER 6

The *Why* Strategy

In an ideal world, each actor in an organization would set aside self-interest and collaborate for the good of the system as a whole, agreeing to share the profits in a reasonable fashion. In theory, it is possible for an organization's culture to be shaped in such a way as to achieve this ideal situation. But when organizations grow larger and more complex, internal fiefdoms and rivalries emerge, making it difficult for culture alone to ensure this collaborative ideal.

That is because the rewards and incentives that determine compensation are designed to motivate types of behavior that advantage the work of each functional area, department, or business unit, and those motivators typically vary from one corner of the business to another. In essence, they define why people do what they do and, often, the way they do it. While rewards and incentives can do a fine job in the context for which they were designed, their very effectiveness will often undermine collaborative work by causing participants to behave in self-interested ways.

This problem can be even more troublesome when multiple firms must work together toward a common objective. The incentives that motivate different organizations pull against each other, and the value chain as a whole suffers. Within a single firm, managers may possess enough leverage to intervene and force the desired give-and-take. But between separate firms, intervention is typically more complicated, marking the difference between working within one tribe and working with two or more whose incentives are not aligned. (See the sidebar, "Why We Do What We Do.")

The purpose of this chapter is to show you how to resolve incentive misalignments by making changes to your business model. We recommend three approaches. The first is to *change the revenue and profit stream* in the transactions between different organizations. You might accomplish this by changing contractual arrangements between parties in your value chain. For example, a traditional contract might involve paying a supplier a fixed amount for provided goods, whereas an innovative contract would tie payment to the quality of the end result (profits and revenues or performance). The second approach is to *synchronize the differing time horizons* imposed by the parties'

Why We Do What We Do

You may have observed firsthand that incentives can work in unpredictable ways. Although we take it on faith that money is the most effective motivator, seemingly weak nonmonetary incentives can be surprisingly effective. For example, simply letting households know how much more electricity they consume than their neighbors can reduce consumption more than monetary incentives.[a] Behavioral economists like Dan Ariely have conducted experiments demonstrating the surprising ways in which people behave irrationally. If you cannot assume that employees will behave rationally in all circumstances, how can you develop incentives that actually work? Ariely, in his book, *Predictably Irrational*, argues that when people behave irrationally, they do so in ways that are both systematic and predictable.[b] Understanding the causes of irrational decisions can suggest ways of producing better ones. But you must always beware the law of unintended consequences. Steven Kerr's seminal 1975 *Academy of Management Journal* article, "On the Folly of Rewarding *A* While Hoping for *B*," still stands as a groundbreaking study on the clumsy design of incentive systems.[c]

a. John Rogers, "Smiley Faces vs. Vampires: Knowledge (About Power) Is Power," *The Equation*, http://blog.ucsusa.org/smiley-faces-vs-vampires-knowledge-about-power-is-power/.

b. Dan Ariely, *Predictably Irrational: The Hidden Forces That Shape Our Decisions*, rev. ed. (New York: HarperCollins, 2010).

c. S. Kerr, "On the Folly of Rewarding *A* While Hoping for *B*," *Academy of Management Journal* 18, no. 4 (1975): 769–783.

respective business models in order to repair misaligned incentives. For example, one organization might care only about a single transaction's immediate gains or losses, while the other is focused on building longer-term value. If both parties commit to an open-ended relationship— one that will encompass many transactions into the fore-seeable future—each develops a mutual interest in the other's sustained long-term success. By syncing their time horizons, both organizations will work for the common good. The third approach covers situations in which the uncertainty is so high that it is not possible to write con-tracts that cover all contingencies or to commit to engag-ing with the other party for the foreseeable future. In such situations, the best (and often only) solution may be to *pur-sue a strategy of vertical integration.*

Redefining the Revenue Model: Performance-Based Contracts

You are quite likely familiar with legendary tales about defense contractors charging the US government absurdly high prices for screwdrivers, toilet seats, and flashlights. To be sure, such nonsensical costs can add up. But there are other, more worrying inefficiencies that arise from tra-ditional contracting methods, and these make the toilet-seat problem seem trivial by comparison.

In the past, when the US Department of Defense (DoD) purchased expensive aircraft, it would agree to a "time and materials" (T&M) arrangement for repairs and regular maintenance. Under T&M, customers are charged for the labor and materials consumed (on a cost-plus basis) in the course of each maintenance event, similar to the way you pay a mechanic for car repairs. It's estimated that for every $1 the government spends to purchase a new airplane, it will spend $7 on T&M charges over the life of the plane. Unfortunately, this model offers no incentive for a contractor to maximize the length of time between service events. Indeed, from the contractor-incentives point of view, under T&M the operating principle for servicing, say, jet engines would be *the more problems, the better.*

If you think back to the Blockbuster example discussed earlier, you see here the same type of incentive misalignment that, in the 1990s, damaged the movie-rental value chain. There was no compelling reason for movie studios to care whether Blockbuster thrived or not, until Sumner Redstone gave them one in the form of a revenue-sharing scheme. Likewise, given the way defense contractors' incentives were structured, jet-engine reliability was not a focal priority, despite the fact that it was extremely important to their military customers. In reality, the less reliable the engines were, the more the contractors' maintenance revenues rose.

This system created an assortment of perverse incentives—and lack of incentives. As a practical matter, for example, contractors had no incentive to pressure their suppliers to increase the quality of engine components, innovate through more efficient designs, use more durable materials, or develop better preventive maintenance strategies. Until, that is, the DoD gave them a reason to care about engine reliability and change why they designed engines the way they did.

In 2004, facing pressure to cut costs and improve performance, the DoD sought a way to change the *why* of the contracting business model. It wanted to align the incentives of contractors around the goals of *lower maintenance cost* and *higher engine reliability* so as to increase aircraft availability and the length of time between service events. It adopted a contracting method called performance-based contracting (PBC). In essence, the objective of PBC was to change the revenue model for contractors. They would be paid for the amount of time the aircraft was actually in service, with the DoD specifying, for example, 95 percent availability as its threshold. As a result, the contractor would earn more the longer a jet engine performed without needing to be taken out of service for maintenance or repair.

The large trend that PBC represents is the "servicization" of what were once straightforward product purchases. Servicization—tying providers' revenues to specific performance thresholds—can be a potent *why* form of business model innovation. It gives the provider a strong incentive to deliver both quality products and services (because better-engineered products require less frequent service). We now see instances where, for example, the owners of large office and apartment buildings pay for heating and air conditioning as a service, based on a contracted level of system uptime (usually 99 percent or higher) or on maintaining a specified temperature.

Performance-based contracting isn't an entirely new approach: the jet-engine division of Rolls-Royce was using a version of it thirty years ago. For a 2009 research project that we and some of our colleagues conducted at the Wharton School, we studied the experience of Rolls-Royce and its commercial aviation customers, looking at service records over a five-year period during which the firm offered buyers a choice between PBC- and T&M-based maintenance contracts.[1] This allowed us to compare both methods' performance outcomes. We found that, on average, the time between engine overhauls was 790 in-service hours longer using the PBC model than under a traditional T&M contract. Depending on how heavily used the customers' aircraft were, PBC delivered a reliability dividend that ranged between 10 percent and 25 percent. (We were unable to make such a side-by-side comparison for defense contracts since the two methods were never simultaneously in use.)

While the advantages of PBC are clearest on the customer side, there is further work to do to understand clearly how contractors might also benefit. A PBC contract in effect transfers resource management risks from customers to contractors (a *who* as well as a *why* change). This makes sense because the contractor has superior information about and control over both its supplier network and its maintenance personnel. But contracting is a complex art, and the ultimate success of the PBC method will depend on formulas to compensate contractors for taking on the added risks.

It's worth noting, however, that part of the harm of T&M also fell on the contractor side, leading to a lack of attention paid to process efficiencies over time. Because contractors had little incentive to operate leanly, they may have overlooked opportunities to address business-model flaws of their own. PBC now gives them a reason to pursue long-neglected innovations. Those greater efficiencies—including in the area of resource management—may, in turn, soften the blow of any decline in maintenance revenues. To be sure, these are long-term relationship issues that need to be negotiated carefully and in good faith.

That said, we believe there are opportunities to apply PBC-like models in a variety of industries. Any business in which the failure of essential equipment would prove costly is a potential candidate for PBC: oil and gas companies, chemical and semiconductor manufacturers, hospitals, cruise lines, financial services firms that execute high-speed trades. In short, if your business relies on equipment that is maintained by an outside party under contract, there may be highly consequential incentive-alignment inefficiencies to address.

CAVEATS: Performance-based contracting works well when performance can be fully and unambiguously defined. For instance, using PBC in developing a new airplane that relies on advanced technologies and materials is unlikely to work because it is difficult to predict reasonable performance standards and develop appropriate metrics; there are simply too many unknown unknowns involved. A supplier asked to bid on such a contract would demand an exceptionally high price in order to compensate for the uncertainties it will encounter. Further, you need to factor in the way PBC might influence customer behavior. Contractors may have to factor in the possibility that PBC customers will subject aircraft engines to heavier than normal use (as our research at Rolls-Royce suggested). It would therefore be helpful if contracts included safeguards defining thresholds for "reasonable" equipment usage.

Aligning Time Horizons in the Global Sourcing Market

In astrophysical terms, we know the world is round, but for most business and economic purposes, we act as if it were flat. Increasing specialization, technological complexity, and globalization have led businesses to obtain myriad products and services from a limitless array of outside providers. In the automotive, consumer electronics, and retail industries, reliably sourcing materials, parts, and finished products from supply chain partners is the key to success. Li & Fung Ltd., one of the world's fastest-growing companies, has fundamentally changed the game in the industries that rely heavily on sourcing.[2] Li & Fung has grown at a compounded annual rate of 23 percent for the past fourteen years to achieve annual sales of more than $20 billion.

Best known for sourcing apparel and toys from the low-cost economies of Asia, the group today operates in an expanding range of categories. It is present in more than forty economies across North America, Europe, and Asia, with a global sourcing network of nearly fifteen thousand international suppliers, as well as thousands of buyers. The company owns no production, transportation, or retail facilities, but it has nonetheless become the key link in the sourcing practices of some of the world's best-known companies. So how has Li & Fung created a multibillion-dollar business while outclassing established champions in the game of sourcing?

Traditional sourcing relies on a variety of competitive-bidding rituals that ensure low prices and moderate but acceptable quality, typically with the sole goal of lowering sourcing costs. The chosen provider wins the business for a short time, at the conclusion of which the bidding process repeats. This model has served many industries well for decades, enduring for as long as sourcing remained a dominantly cost-driven undertaking.

But as the use of overseas sourcing increased, with it came undercurrents of reputational risk. Faraway suppliers sometimes cut corners on quality control and materials reliability. Worse, there were the occasional unsavory revelations of abusive labor practices (including child-labor violations), product diversion, and the production of counterfeit goods. But since most sourcing transactions were one-off deals—with today's low bidder being replaced by a new one tomorrow—shoddy providers faced few consequences. Until, of course, multinationals felt the corrosive impact that repeated performance problems began to have on their brands. At that point, the short-term time horizon of the provider firms' business model became the focus of *why* attention.

Li & Fung exploited the relational advantages of intermediation to create a new business model based on combining *the flexibility of competitive sourcing* with the *confidence of long-term relationships*. It had absorbed the lesson of Toyota, which came to dominate the automotive industry largely on the strength of its long-term supplier relationships. The Toyota Production System abandoned traditional competitive bidding, preferring instead to enter into long-term partnerships with suppliers.

These partnerships involved substantial cross-ownership arrangements, in which Toyota made irreversible investments in such relationship-specific assets as co-located plants and integrated IT systems. Each of these commitments increased suppliers' confidence that the relationship with Toyota was designed to last, rather than subject to the whims of periodic bidding rituals.

Li & Fung saw that it could add unique value by innovating a new global sourcing ecosystem based on intermediation. It would occupy the point of leverage between multinationals and sourcing providers. From that intermediary position, it provides sourcing services to major brands and retailers worldwide, including Walmart, Target, Zara, and Levi-Strauss. Typically, Li & Fung takes over the client's sourcing function. It selects, verifies, and approves suppliers; allocates business between or among different suppliers; and manages the client's relationship with each supplier—including by crafting incentives for investments (in people, facilities, and materials), performance, and compliance.

You might wonder why it makes sense to add new channel members when each entrant takes yet another piece of the pie. The answer is that Li & Fung optimizes the channel's value and efficiency by reducing all channel members' risks, including, but not limited to, information and incentive-alignment risks. For example, as the main interface between buyers and suppliers, Li & Fung exerts important control over risks relating to product quality, logistics (transport and timely delivery), and financial payments, among others.

The key to this business model is that Li & Fung and other similar firms enter into long-term sourcing arrangements with both buyers and suppliers, matching needs to capabilities. Having long-term relationships with other value-chain partners changes the horizons of the participants as they make their decisions. In short-term relationships, partners have no incentive to think of long-term outcomes. But with greater confidence in the longevity of a relationship, partners begin to focus on building long-term value.

Creating a shared time horizon for buyers and providers brings their incentives into alignment. These phenomena are well known to economists. Once there is the possibility of repeated long-term interaction among different parties, self-interest focuses on building and sustaining value. Everyone can be better off.

Within its network of buyers and suppliers, Li & Fung can change the suppliers that are matched to different buyers at any point. This provides a modicum of flexibility while maintaining uninterrupted relationships with different buyers and sellers.[3] Essentially, sourcing for multiple buyers allows an intermediary like Li & Fung the flexibility to choose which suppliers are best suited to be matched with which buyers. At the same time, all suppliers are guaranteed to receive a healthy stream of orders from the network of Li & Fung buyers, thus ensuring that relationships endure.

CAVEATS: Aligning the time horizons of different players works best when the long-term effects on value creation are most critical. This is often the case when the consequences of different parties' actions are not easily discerned in the short run. (In the automobile industry, the reliability of supplied parts is a good example.) In addition, Li & Fung—and other firms that provide comparable services—are few and far between. If your firm pursues sourcing activities in sectors or regions where you lack recourse to a trusted intermediary, you will need to manage such relationships directly. With little flexibility to switch easily from one supplier to another, you will need to watch out for incentive misalignments and be prepared to intervene to correct them. Be aware, too, that building long-term buyer-supplier relationships will be difficult if management, on either side, remains more focused on short-term goals. Among other things, such a mismatch could threaten the sorts of irreversible—and sometimes risky—mutual investments that ensure a long-term commitment between firms.

In the next section, we look at situations where the effects of partners' actions are indiscernible even in the long run. In such cases, aligning time horizons offers little benefit. Instead, you must change the system in more fundamental ways.

When Integration Is the Cure for a Broken System

Activities that businesses used to do for themselves are now routinely entrusted to third parties, as in the example Li & Fung's management of many global companies' sourcing needs. Comparable specialist firms manage tasks as diverse as travel services, payroll, IT support, parts of the HR function, security, customer service, and janitorial work.

Often this fragmentation makes good economic sense, but it also comes at a price. Many of the outside firms that have become part of your business ecosystem are governed by different objectives and incentives than those that define your firm. All of those divergently motivated systems may have introduced unforeseen inefficiencies into your business. Doubtless, some of these inefficiencies may be addressed using the *why* approaches described in the previous two sections. However, there are circumstances under which even well-designed contracts won't resolve incentive-alignment inefficiencies. In that case, the only recourse is through vertical integration. Take health care, for example.

Health care is a many-headed monster that businesses have been trying to tame ever since it became part of the benefits structure and a major component of business cost. In the United States, a whopping 17.6 percent of GDP is spent annually on health care.[4] But even though it outspends all other countries by a wide margin, an infamous

World Health Organization study, conducted in 2000, ranked US health care thirty-seventh in terms of quality.[5] And it is not alone: study after study finds that health-care spending around the world is not producing improved health by any measure—whether in longer life spans, lower infant mortality, or higher-quality outcomes.

In the United States, in particular, the roots of the problem are in the business model, not in the failure of technology or physician skills. Indeed, the US health-care model—in which separate components of the system function almost as adversaries—is a disorderly tangle of information risks and misaligned incentives. While many countries have adopted state-run or single-payer health care, the US system remains highly disaggregated. Although myriad private hospitals and insurers give it the appearance of a market, the system as a whole operates without economic transparency, true competition, or evidence-based data that would help patients make informed choices or exercise bargaining power.

Let's look at the business model typical of most employer-provided health-care systems in the United States.[6] The US health-care system consists of mainly independent physicians, hospitals where physicians have admitting privileges, nurses, researchers, technicians, and administrators. Besides those who directly deliver health care, there are the patients and their employers, along with various insurance companies, and the government—in short, the consumers, the payers, and the regulators. And there is a system of reimbursements that determines how much the insurer or the government, or both, will pay for each procedure performed by a provider.

In terms of business model inefficiencies, how does this play out in practice? Inefficiencies typically cluster around the two fundamental business model decisions.

What Treatment Should Be Prescribed for a Patient?

The health-care system is dominantly structured to *diagnose and treat illness* rather than to *sustain wellness*. Doctors are paid when patients are sick, not healthy (not unlike the DoD suppliers paid under T&M contracts). This causes a systemic incentive-alignment risk. Doctors make more money when they prescribe more procedures, needed or not. Consequently, physicians are rewarded for taking a short-term view of the patient's health. The weight of incentives imposed by the business model emphasizes treating the patient's current condition rather than preventing some future condition.

How Should Treatment Be Priced and Paid For?

Employers sign agreements with insurance companies to provide coverage for employees; insurance companies, in turn, sign agreements with area hospitals and physician practices. The idea behind these agreements is to build leverage to negotiate volume discounts: employers in order to get favorable rates from insurers, and insurers to get favorable rates from hospitals and physicians. In reality, hospitals and specialist physicians frequently set rates for procedures, tests, and therapies that are many times higher than the cost to provide them. As a result, even plans that have negotiated the most favorable discounts are likely to reimburse hospitals and physicians for much more than the cost of delivering prescribed care.

The forces that operate on all of the system's parties lead to a high degree of perversity. On the patient side, perversity manifests as information risk; on the provider side, it is mainly a matter of incentive-alignment risk:

- Patients, who make decisions based on profound information inefficiencies, must trust the judgment, skill, and experience of their physicians. And, in most cases, even if they had sufficient information, they would be hard-pressed to remain objective in what are sometimes life-or-death situations. If a specialist orders an MRI, what patient would ask for an X-ray instead? And, as a rule, patients don't usually know what care costs until after it's been provided.

- Hospitals, which have invested in expensive diagnostic and treatment technologies, have an incentive to use those tools as often as possible, to the point of turning every MRI or CT scanner into a profit center. Because teaching hospitals combine the missions of physician training, research, and patient care, they are especially prone to incentive misalignments when teaching and research activities conflict with patient-care priorities.

- Physicians have an incentive to prescribe MRIs instead of X-rays, since doing so is financially rewarding both for them and for the institutions with which they affiliate. Besides, patients always want the best available technology. Patients also want the latest medications. This makes physicians easy targets for drug-marketing strategies that could compromise their objectivity (such as, for example, when physicians are rewarded by drug companies to prescribe their medications more than those of competitors).

- Insurers—as long as they can raise premiums, hold down administrative costs, demand higher patient deductibles, and deny enough claims—have no incentive to question the economics that govern the system they've helped create. Doing so could open a can of worms that might threaten their role in the system.

- Drug companies have incentives to prefer the status quo. The US health-care model has provided them with the world's highest prescription drug prices. They enjoy a reasonably tolerant regulatory environment that allows them, within reason, to market drugs for off-label uses.

Businesses, like individual patients, struggle to control what they can in a system that often defies reason. Consequently, they have few options to make genuine headway against problems of such magnitude manifested on so many fronts.

So what is the possible solution? Part of what ails the current health-care model is the constant tension between disaggregated parties motivated by different objectives and incentives. The problem is disaggregation. Possibly the best way to align the incentives of all parties so that they work toward the shared goal of sustaining wellness is by integrating doctors, hospitals, employees, and employers *in a single organization*. Since employers and employees pay the lion's share of health-care costs, integrating some or all of the system of care into business enterprises brings the parties together around the clear focal objective of keeping the pool of insured people as healthy as possible and thereby driving down costs—both now and in the future. Incentives would reward an emphasis on maintaining wellness over treating sickness. Investments in wellness are inexpensive compared with the cost of treating ailments; since many ailments are avoidable through changes in behavior, the long-term focus pays enormous dividends.

Physicians, like everyone else, would be salaried employees of the company. As long as they and others in the system are incented toward the goal of better employee health, there would be no conflict of interest. (To be sure, employees' privacy interests with respect to their health records would have to be earnestly protected.) The company would have to be self-insured to avoid ceding decision-making power to an insurer with its own profit agenda.

Adventures in Integration

The idea of integrating health care may seem utopian, but a growing number of innovative US companies have begun bringing it to life with encouraging success.[7] Quad/Graphics, a large printing company with annual revenues of more than $4 billion, implemented such a system and lowered its health-care costs by an estimated 30 percent. Perdue Farms, Sprint, and Pitney-Bowes have done likewise. Perdue employs twenty-six doctors and operates its own laboratory, pharmacy, and rehabilitative care facility. These companies all contract with hospitals for advanced care requiring expensive equipment, but such cases are a small fraction of the total care employees consume. The firms' self-insurance programs are equipped to handle situations that involve treating very sick employees.

Ensuring good outcomes requires not just shifting responsibility for health-care decisions to internal doctors, but also tying doctors' bonuses to patient evaluations, early intervention strategies for disease prevention, and positive health outcomes. These sorts of metrics are far more clearly correlated with long-term health than the number of procedures a physician orders. The success of Quad/Graphics' in-house health program has led it to begin operating clinics for other companies. Quad spends much more money on preventive medicine than on hospital costs, which appears to demonstrate that the system reduced alignment inefficiency in the right direction. For example, the rate of Caesarian section births among women in the Quad health-care system is only 12 percent, compared with 26 percent nationally. Given the debate about the overprescription of Caesarian sections by doctors, this is a remarkable result and one that clearly translates into cost savings.[8]

Taken as a whole, the trend toward providing health-maintenance care for employees has produced encouraging results. For instance, Freddie Mac found that a clinic that costs $600,000 per year to run adds roughly $900,000 a year in increased employee productivity.[9] The ultimate goal of these types of initiatives is to produce healthier employees and healthier balance sheets.

The US health-care system as a whole presents what is often called a "wicked problem"—one whose complexities,

CAVEATS: Needless to say, vertical integration is not a trivial task. Many organizations rightly hesitate to reverse the trend of fragmentation in order to take on directly performing activities that are outside their core competencies. (The fact that more businesses are doing so is evidence of some desperation to find a better way.) An alternative to becoming direct health-care providers might be to approach the problem through contract design, much as Blockbuster did in its revenue-sharing contracts with movie studios. Under what is called a *gain-sharing* arrangement, physicians would share the benefits from health-care cost reductions. (Employees, too, could share gains when they engage in successful wellness strategies.) Unfortunately, in the United States, gain-sharing contracts with health-care providers can raise legal issues. Laws prohibit efforts to motivate physicians through incentives that would reduce medical services.[10] Nevertheless, the US government has granted some legal waivers for experiments designed to test the potential benefits of gain sharing. These have produced some encouraging results.[11] Yet another promising contracting approach is the *bundled payment model* that reimburses providers on the basis of expected costs for episodes of care.[12] But for both of these contracting approaches, there are aspects of the cause-and-effect equation that defy scientific observation and control, and therefore cannot be contracted. Many long-term medical outcomes fall into the class of gains that are difficult to account for in a contract. In such cases, integration can be a potentially promising remedy for businesses. But because of integration's higher degree of difficulty and investment, it should only be done in circumstances for which the other two *why* innovation approaches are inadequate.

interdependencies, and internal contradictions and tensions make it especially resistant to solutions. That businesses in growing numbers have embraced these sorts of in-house experiments shows the extent of frustration with a system that is both out of control and seems focused on the wrong approaches. US businesses have historically been invested in employee health care through the insurance benefits they offer. Moreover, employees in recent years have paid a growing share of insurance costs. Businesses may not have anticipated what they were in for when they first took on the burden of employee health care, but now they're beginning to recognize the value of seizing control of the delivery system more directly.

TAKEAWAYS

At the heart of the *why* approach to business model innovation is the key insight that organizations make decisions because they are driven by incentives that often differ from those of other parties in the value chain. Based on this insight, there are three ways of changing a flawed business model:

Change the revenue model to align incentives. Very often, the cause of misaligned incentives is simply a poorly designed relationship (or contract) between companies, one that may exist for reasons of historical practice. In these cases, a shift to performance-based contracting often eliminates perverse incentives.

Replace short-term relationships with long-term partnerships. Incentive-alignment risk arises when organizations have different time horizons. A supplier whose decision making is based on short-term incentives for cost reduction will cut corners in ways that undercut the long-term value proposition. Aligning everyone's incentives around long-term relationships usually focuses all parties on building value that can endure.

Integrate. Some business models drive so much complexity that the best way to reduce misalignments is to bring the disparate parties together in a single organization. When guided by clearly focused objectives and motivated by compatible incentives, an integrated enterprise will produce superior outcomes at a lower cost. But high cost and high difficulty make it a last resort.

Why Innovation in Action—P2P Car Sharing: From Napster to Relay Rides

Why would you rent your shiny new car to a complete stranger for a few dollars an hour? What if he or she does not treat it with the same love and care that you do? What if he or she doesn't have a great driving record or runs up some speeding and parking tickets? Why would you—as a renter—make sure that there are no parking tickets on a car you borrowed from a stranger? At worst, he will not rent you his car again, but there are perhaps plenty of other fish in the sea.

These concerns have limited the spread of peer-to-peer (p2p) car sharing. The peer-to-peer model that was widely successful for sharing reproducible digital goods via the internet (think Napster, uTorrent, and the like) has not made much of a mark beyond the digital realm, despite the obvious utilization efficiencies of sharing physical goods such as cars. A whole host of promising p2p car-sharing start-ups, best exemplified by Relay Rides, are planning to change all that by innovating the *why* of the rental and the use decision. While renters leasing from other individuals may have no reason to take care of the car, an intermediary (akin to Li & Fung, which we described earlier) can take these one-off lessee-lessor transactions and make them into long-standing relationships that both the lessor and the lessee have with the intermediary. Now a renter who "misbehaves" will not just lose the use of one car, but may be banned from the platform itself, fundamentally changing his incentives to take care of the vehicle. Moreover, it is easier for such a marketplace to create a reliable, boilerplate contract that each user must adhere to and that can be used as a last resort to align incentives. This is exactly what p2p marketplace enablers like Relay Rides are trying to do. Inserting intermediaries into the equation changes the horizon of relationships, which alters *why* decisions to offer cars for rental and decisions on how to use rental cars are made. Will they succeed in making p2p car sharing as frictionless as downloading a movie on the internet? Only time will tell.

In our final chapter, we turn our attention to BMI implementation, using a case study to show how even inexperienced hands can produce a successful business model with surprising speed.

CHAPTER 7

Business Model Innovation in Action

Although we have described many examples of business model innovation in our book, we have yet to show the full trajectory of a project, from the original rough idea to an emerging concept, to the rounds of iterative experimentation that help shape the concept into a workable business model, followed by its early success in the market and eventual evolution as business conditions change.

This chapter's main component is an effort to fill in some of the blanks. It is the story of TerraPass, a start-up venture that grew out of an MBA class one of us taught at the Wharton School of Business in 2004.[1]

Although TerraPass is far from being our greatest success, we like it for a number of reasons. First, we learned a lot from it; it was a teaching prototype, our first stab at having a class develop a new business and a new business model. Second, it was highly innovative in both strategic and operational ways. Third, the original model benefited from a high degree of experimentation and later mutated as the business matured and coped with sundry challenges.

Finally, and most important for our purposes here, the success of this modest venture—with no money, corporate backing, or seasoned staff—really opened our eyes to the power of business model innovation. It showed how a group of smart people with no prior experience executing BMI projects could apply an early prototype of our framework to innovate—within a matter of weeks—a new business that successfully overcame multiple inefficiencies in an existing market. TerraPass went on to win funding and media attention. It grew—bringing in more than $3 million in annual revenues by late 2006—and was eventually acquired. TerraPass still exists, and although it encountered its share of challenges and continued to tweak its business model, it fulfills much the same mission as it did from the beginning. We will describe how Terra-Pass transformed the market's dominant decision pattern to remediate the inefficiencies it caused.

First, however, we want to introduce you to a tool called the business model innovation matrix (see table 7-1). We use it regularly when working with clients and find it helpful in sorting through many possible innovations.

TABLE 7-1

Business model innovation matrix

What	When	Who	Why
Select focused versus flexible business model.	Delay decisions as much as possible.	Transfer decisions to best-informed players.	Change the profit or revenue streams to align incentives.
Change the scope of decisions.	Change the sequence of decisions.	Transfer decision rights to the party best able to tolerate the consequences.	Synchronize the differing time horizons.
Hedge or complement decisions with each other.	Split decisions to obtain partial information before the decision is completed.	Move the consequences (costs) of the decision to the party that benefits the most.	Pursue a strategy of vertical integration.

Although most readers will likely apply this tool in established businesses, it has also proven to be quite valuable to entrepreneurs launching ventures that disrupt an industry's usual way of doing business (what TerraPass did). We think of the matrix as an "idea trigger" because it offers a quick way to scan the four W levers and twelve innovation approaches, as described in the previous four chapters, and zero in on those likely to be most productive. In that sense, it's a kind of cheat sheet for the contents of the book: somewhere among its dozen cells, you will find the best path for taking your business model in a new direction.

What makes the BMI matrix an effective idea trigger is that it embodies the lessons of hundreds of examples, including each of those we have used here. All of the examples helped shape our thinking, to the point where we would be hard-pressed to come up with a business model problem or opportunity to which none of these twelve innovations could be applied. Indeed, more than one potential approach will frequently emerge.

As we noted earlier, some of the strategies we recommend are familiar ones, first proposed by other business thinkers. The main advantage of our framework is not that it invents completely new rules of business. Rather, its strength lies in viewing business model innovation systematically, through the lens of risk-induced inefficiencies. Our focus has always been to work backward from identified inefficiencies to propose the innovations needed to fix them. That should be your focus, too.

Each cell of the matrix is tailored to particular circumstances, risks, and inefficiencies. For example, looking at the "what" column, note the hedging strategy in the bottom cell. If your firm engages in lines of business that are subject to highly volatile demand, you might find it desirable to hedge the information risks of complementary decisions against each other, as LAN Airlines does by carrying cargo shipments on passenger planes. Also in the "what" column, if your business offers a wide selection of complex products within its category, how might you change the scope of decisions caused by that complexity? As Volkswagen does, you could engineer components to be shared across multiple models.

Although certain types of inefficiency might be more prevalent in some businesses than in others—for instance, every retailer must overcome some level of information risk in predicting how much of which goods to carry— our twelve varieties of innovation should be seen as fully transportable across industries. Just because we may have used examples from industries other than the one in which your firm competes, don't assume that the under- lying mechanisms can't be adapted to your purposes.

Once you've identified the highest-priority BMI chal- lenge to take on—and assuming your team has been trained in the use of the four W's framework—you are ready to use the BMI matrix to prospect for the type of innovation best suited to your circumstances.

TerraPass

In essence, prospecting for innovation is what the students who developed the TerraPass business model did.[2] Dur- ing a six-week class, we trained them in the fundamentals of business model innovation and then put them to work on the challenge of using it to create a new business. We also provided them with a set of principles to guide them

Five Implementation Principles

We recommended that our class of Wharton MBA students follow a set of basic design principles distilled mainly from our work with clients:

- That using well-designed, systematic methods increases the odds that a series of fortunate events will produce a disruptive new business model.

- That it is important to generate ideas for many possible innovations before winnowing them to those most promising.[a]

- That you must use hard data to help refine and evaluate innovation opportunities, eliminating the least attractive ideas quickly and cheaply.

- That it is vital to engage aggressively in experiments designed to help resolve critical uncertainties and unknowns likely to influence business model performance.

- That different tasks demand different types and sizes of teams; depending on the goal, a platoon is often better than a brigade, and vice versa.

That final principle deserves added emphasis. Two types of tasks are required in order to generate, select, and refine innovation opportunities: those that benefit from inputs provided by *a wide group of diverse participants*, and those best accomplished when divided up among *small, empowered committees* working in parallel. It is important to assign the right participants—and the right level of participation—to the right tasks.

a. For an explanation of why generating many opportunities is better than focusing on just one, see Christian Terwiesch and Karl Ulrich, *Innovation Tournaments: Creating and Selecting Exceptional Opportunities* (Boston: Harvard Business School Press, 2009).

(see the sidebar, "Five Implementation Principles"). What ultimately resulted was a business model built primarily on a *who* innovation (with a side dish of *why* thrown in). TerraPass would help individuals concerned about carbon emissions participate in the market for voluntary carbon offsets in order to *indirectly* reduce their environmental impact.

The rest of this chapter tells the story of how TerraPass was developed and how to relate its lessons to your own BMI challenges.

A Carbon-Footprint Problem

In the fall of 2004, Karl Ulrich and Karan Girotra taught a course in developing new business models to a class of forty-one MBA candidates. Ulrich (currently the vice dean of innovation at Wharton) was a committed environmentalist, but he was having a little problem with his carbon footprint. At the time, he was driving a pickup truck back and forth between Philadelphia and Vermont, where he was building a home. He needed a truck not only for transportation but to haul building materials to the home site. He faced a predicament that many others do as well: although he didn't then have the option to either drive less or drive a more fuel-efficient vehicle, he wished that there was a simple way to compensate for his personal environmental impact. Ulrich thought his uneasy conscience might be a good starting point for a new business model.

The students began the project with only a broad, general idea: to address in some way the environmental impact of carbon emissions from driving cars, SUVs, and light trucks. After learning the framework, they had the remaining weeks of the course and $5,000 in seed money to create a business that would provide a workable solution for drivers concerned about carbon emissions. They would have to operate within this limited budget and time frame, and employ a systematic process of development, refinement, experimentation, and testing. We expected that their final output would successfully address the problem of carbon emissions through a business model innovation rather than a traditional R&D-style innovation involving new technology.

The students were probably extra-motivated, knowing that their professor had a personal stake in whatever solution they ultimately produced. Among the earliest parameters that emerged during the class's brainstorming was that, for a variety of reasons, people like Ulrich cannot easily change their driving habits. Insights of this kind helped narrow down the W options. If the team's business model had to satisfy people who couldn't change their driving habits, perhaps they could change something else. After all, many activities—heating, cooling, using electric lights and other appliances—contribute to a household's carbon footprint.

Thus, one of the early proposals was to develop an online "energy-efficiency adviser" application. Most people have no idea how to measure their aggregate environmental impact. Their overall behavior is therefore subject to high information risk. This *who* innovation proposed transferring the task of analyzing behavior to an outside party. Individuals and families could go to a website, complete a comprehensive questionnaire, and get an analysis of their entire carbon profile that identified opportunities to reduce other carbon-producing activities. While this seemed like a good idea for a government agency or an advocacy group to pursue—perhaps as part of an overall education and awareness campaign—the students concluded that it lacked the plausible revenue model that would make it a promising business.

Another idea sought to better align incentives so that individuals would be more motivated to change their behavior in nondriving areas of their carbon production. In a proposed membership model, a business would accept commitments from individuals to reduce their overall carbon impact by an amount equivalent to their vehicles' emissions—say ten tons per year. At the start of the year, a member would pay $100. If she successfully reduced carbon impact in other areas by a full ten tons, she would get $100 back; if by three tons, she would get back only $30. The model's *why* innovation creates an incentive for direct reductions through changes in behavior. The more successful members are at changing their behavior, the larger the rebate. (All programs geared to motivate behavioral changes—think of Weight Watchers and other self-improvement programs—depend on models with a *why* innovation at their core.)

In the *what* category was an idea to assemble a broad investment portfolio of carbon-reducing projects in different areas (solar, wind, geothermal, energy efficiency, and so on). Instead of investing in single projects, individuals buy shares in the entire fund. The fund's breadth and diversity allow complementary decisions to hedge one another's results. If one project fails to produce anticipated benefits, another will likely overperform. The key to this idea is in creating the complementarity required to hedge the risk associated with any single investment.

There were many other ideas, including some related to bicycles: a project to develop automated bike-rental kiosks in urban areas, such as those that have lately become common in many European and US cities; and a civic-minded campaign to encourage more bicycle commuting from the nearby Philadelphia neighborhoods and suburbs. While these were all interesting, some (such as the bike kiosks) were too expensive to develop, and others were complicated and rife with uncertainty or else simply not viable as ongoing businesses. Nor did they necessarily address Ulrich's predicament: the need to compensate for his carbon impact without changing the main aspect of his carbon-producing lifestyle.

However, another of the ideas put forward suggested an intriguing kind of online business: a website that would raise seed money for an assortment of greenhouse-gas-reducing projects. In some respects, this was an idea that anticipated Kickstarter, the popular *when* decision-splitting innovation that we described in chapter 4. The premise of the idea was that there must be plenty of environmental entrepreneurs looking for just enough investment money to investigate the potential of their projects or product ideas. Why not invite them to test the waters on a green-focused website where environmental sinners came to invest in worthy ventures that would offset their carbon impact?

Like many good ideas that are nonetheless not quite right, this one pointed in an interesting direction: toward the existing market for trading in carbon offsets. Given their limited time and budget, the students' discussions increasingly focused on making expedient choices—to wit, why waste time inventing something that already exists?

Overall, we had nearly twenty-five possible approaches to the broad challenge of creating a business model that would facilitate carbon reductions for concerned individuals who were unable to achieve such reductions directly. The entire group of forty-one students had been involved in the ideation process. Together—after debating and challenging the key assumptions underlying each idea—we voted on the output, overwhelmingly favoring the proposal to build a business around the trading of carbon offsets.

Looking for Flaws in the Existing Model

As the students began to look at the carbon-offset market, they learned that there were actually two distinct markets. The larger of these exists to facilitate compliance with *mandatory* carbon-reduction targets driven by national, regional, and international regulatory regimes (such as the Kyoto Protocols); a second, much smaller segment consists of *voluntary* offset purchases, generally involving environmentally conscious individuals and small to mid-sized businesses. The voluntary market was served by a few trading bodies, the largest of which is the Chicago Carbon Exchange (CCX). It was the voluntary market that the students sought to leverage. Obviously, mandatory carbon-reduction targets don't apply to the Karl Ulrichs of the world (though the day may come when they will).

The way both offset markets work is by creating a mechanism that allows polluters to pay for their sins. If a business is unwilling or unable to invest in capital improvements aimed at reducing its emissions directly, it can pay a sum of money that goes toward developing new greenhouse-gas-reducing initiatives to be executed by others. In return, the buyer receives credits equivalent to a specific amount of carbon reduction that goes toward off-setting its own emissions. In essence, industrial purchasers of offsets are paying proxies to reduce greenhouse gases so that they can continue to pollute. In both offset markets, there are exchanges that facilitate the trading of investments for credits. For example, the CCX is a classic cap-and-trade model where net polluters purchase credits from net reducers.

Since a market for carbon offsets already existed, couldn't individuals successfully and efficiently participate in it? The students learned that the answer to that question was yes and no. It was true that individuals weren't barred from buying voluntary offsets, but the market imposed two key disincentives:

- Would-be participants faced a significant entry barrier: a membership fee that amounted to a few thousand dollars. In effect, this upfront payment merely got them into the game. People with thousands of dollars to spend on carbon reduction typically purchased a hybrid or electric vehicle instead. Or they bought replacement windows and installed extra insulation in their homes.

- It was difficult for an individual offset buyer to evaluate the quality of particular investment options. Among the main criteria for judging offsets' quality was whether they would truly produce *new* carbon reductions—what is referred to as "additionality"—or would instead have happened in any case. Additionality was imperative. If purchased offsets failed the additionality test, the credits would be worthless. Although the exchanges made some effort to vet their offerings, it was not a perfect art, and investments sometimes proved to be defective. Buyers typically had to fend for themselves.

There is little practical difference between analyzing the strengths and weaknesses of business models in a single organization and analyzing those that are prevalent across an industry, since each firm's business model tends to reflect the industry's competitive realities. Nearly every new business is launched as a direct assault upon the flaws and inefficiencies of an existing model. So, the same general rules apply: follow the risks to the inefficiencies they create, and then work back from the inefficiencies to the best way of eliminating them.

That is the approach the students took. Each of the two disincentives to individual participation in the offset market revealed inefficiencies based on our two characteristic types of risk:

- **Incentive-alignment risk.** Because it was scaled primarily for businesses, the voluntary market's revenue model was misaligned with the interests of individual buyers, who had little incentive to pay an entry fee that was probably far in excess of the impact of their actual carbon emissions. Some way had to be found to align the interests of this customer segment with those of the market.

- **Information risk.** The difficulty individual consumers faced in acquiring complete and accurate information about the quality of particular offset options left them in the dark, especially when judging whether projects met the additionality standard.

In terms of their effect on customer behavior, the two risks actually amplified each other: The dramatically high minimum entry price raised the stakes of judging offset quality, and the difficulty of reliably judging quality made the high entry price completely intolerable.

From the insights the students had gleaned about voluntary offsets, we developed some rough BMI design criteria:

1. Carbon-reducing offsets didn't need to be expensive to be effective.[3]

2. Purchasing offsets didn't need to be difficult or complicated.

3. Purchasers needed a basis for feeling confident that offsets would deliver the intended benefits.

4. A proposed new business could play a useful intermediary role in helping to ensure easy access to carefully evaluated carbon offsets.

Finding the Right W

As the examples in chapter 5 demonstrate, sometimes you need a third party to decide for you something that you either cannot or should not decide for yourself. *Who* innovations therefore focus on finding the best available alternative (in terms of information and incentives) to handle the circumstances you face. Since the mission of our class was to launch that third-party alternative, it had the latitude to design the ideal solution for both of the problems presented by the identified risk-driven inefficiencies.

The team enumerated the various *who* aspects that needed to be dealt with. First, of course, prospective Terra-Pass customers needed efficient access to qualified proxies able to compensate for their vehicles' carbon emissions. Second, they needed third-party expertise to make sound judgments about which particular offsets were likeliest to deliver *additional* carbon reductions in the most efficient way. Third, they needed a deep-pocketed intermediary able to invest in carbon-reducing projects (either directly with project owners or through an exchange) so that the cost of a large number of offsets could be sliced into relatively inexpensive portions suitable for individual vehicle owners. (It is this third aspect that accounts for the subordinate *why* innovation. Without a mechanism for creating a price structure that was rationally linked to actual vehicle emissions, the model would not solve the incentive alignment inefficiency that precluded participation by most individuals.)

The team identified two innovations from the "Who" column in table 7-1:

1. TerraPass would address the information risk associated with vetting offset options for quality and additionality by transferring decisions to the best-informed party: itself. TerraPass would decide which offsets to buy. It would both partner with the Chicago Carbon Exchange and would also, in some cases, deal directly with the owners of carbon-reducing projects. This was an important benefit. In some quarters, carbon offsets were controversial because claims of additional carbon reductions sometimes turned out to be shaky. By making direct investments in remediation projects—applying an extra layer of due diligence on customers' behalf rather than depending solely on the CCX—TerraPass strengthened validation and credibility.

2. Because TerraPass was the party that stood to benefit most if the business thrived, it designed its model to absorb the financial consequences of purchasing large numbers of offsets. While this, too, was purely a *who* innovation, it necessitated a

Putting a Price on Carbon

After researching the economics of carbon reduction, the students came to understand that if a single individual were able to invest in a low-priced offset, she could far more economically reduce greenhouse gas emissions than by purchasing a hybrid vehicle (at a cost of as much as $10,000 more than a conventional one). For example, based on 2004 carbon pricing, a relatively small offset investment—something in the $10 to $20 range—could deliver a carbon-reduction benefit roughly comparable to driving a hybrid vehicle for a year. That insight put the traditional carbon-exchange model's entry price of thousands of dollars in a new light. By comparison, building a rational pricing model for TerraPass ought to be easy.

The consumer research team wanted to set a price in a way that related logically to the types of cars offset purchasers drove. After testing price points, this is where they settled: owners of the least fuel-efficient cars (ten to sixteen miles per gallon) would pay $79.95 annually to remediate ten tons of carbon; those with cars in the middle (seventeen to twenty-four

supporting *why* innovation: changing the profit and revenue streams to align incentives. Ultimately, this led the consumer research team to develop a three-tiered pricing scheme based on the average fuel consumption of different types of vehicles. The students concluded that even the largest of gas guzzlers could offset their carbon miles per gallon) would pay $49.95 to remediate six tons; and owners of the most fuel-efficient cars (more than twenty-five miles per gallon) would pay $39.95 to remediate four tons. The team later added a lower-priced ($29.95) fourth tier for hybrid vehicles, which accounted for 8 percent of sales. (The vehicle classes' respective price points assumed a volume of annual carbon emissions based on twelve thousand miles of average driving distance.)

The pledge to customers was that offsets purchased at those price points would be proportional to their cars' actual yearly environmental impact. The pricing scheme was a breakthrough in terms of expanding access to carbon offsets by making them affordable. It also had the virtues of being simple and easy to understand, and of incorporating a reasonably accurate way of relating each price point to a level of carbon impact. (By comparison, TerraPass's only competitor, a nonprofit called The Carbon Fund, required its would-be customers to provide detailed answers to questions about their vehicles and their driving habits. This added a potentially offputting—and unnecessary— layer of administrative overkill.)

emissions for an annual fee of less than $100 (see the sidebar, "Putting a Price on Carbon").

Using Small Teams for Specialized Tasks

Beyond a certain point—typically when tasks become increasingly differentiated—a large group is cumbersome and inefficient. The ideation phase described happened in the early part of the course. Once the initial concept had been reasonably well defined, the group split into small teams (each consisting of three or four members) focused on different aspects of developing the idea. Table 7-2 is a partial list of the types of activities various subgroups began working on. Note that this list of tasks is not necessarily chronological. For example, the product design team needed input from the three teams below it on the list in order to complete its job effectively. There also had to be clear and ongoing communication between some teams more than others. For example, the product design and brand management teams needed to collaborate closely.

Given the structure and economics of the voluntary offset market, it was clear to our students where the inefficiencies lay. The good news was that the idea of building a business to facilitate offset trading by individuals had clear potential. The challenges lay in how to overcome the existing model's main risks and how to conceive a strategy for marketing the new business model's value proposition to the customer segments most likely to be receptive to it. To our delight (since it affirmed the utility of our emerging framework), the team discovered that the former challenge would be easier to address than the latter.

TABLE 7-2

Teams and tasks

Team name	Possible roles, tasks, decisions	Mission-critical deliverable(s)
Product design	• Physical product concept • Product design • Product specifications • Product architecture	• Detail design of first product released to production • Organize design competition
Business development	• Partner identification or evaluation • Short list of three to five partners to approach • Develop proposals • Pitch to prospective partners	• One to three prime candidates • Establish dialogue
Certification and science	• White paper on consumer offsets • Mechanisms for trust • Analysis of offsets • Certify organizations	• Credible white paper • Certification for website
Supply chain management—offsets	• Identify offset suppliers • Evaluate suppliers • Select or establish supply • Cost model for supply	• Offset source in place
Brand management	• Corporate identity • Brand identity • Brand image • Brand message • Website brand or company content	• Brand: oversee name competition • Graphic identity • Tag line • Website content regarding company
Public relations	• Identify media targets • Develop pitches • Events and tie-ins • Press releases	• Promote "classroom project" as a news story
Fulfillment, customer relationship management, customer service	• Fulfillment process design • CRM systems, database • Customer-service mechanisms • Order fulfillment • Sales force integration	• Fulfillment system in place • Customer service system • Customer database
Consumer research	• Develop segmentation model • Predict consumer demand • Uncover core drivers of purchases • Identify alternatives in consideration set • Estimate price sensitivity	• Segmentation model • Pricing model • Benefits • Forecast

Experiments in Marketing

As we have noted, one of the virtues of business model innovation is its economy. You are building value out of inexpensive materials, consisting mainly of people's time and creative energy, and most of the investments go toward iterative experiments that either succeed or provide value in the lessons of a quick failure. That's a good thing under any circumstances, but it's decisively important—even with a workforce of unpaid students—when your launch budget is only $5,000.

Almost every aspect of developing a new product (or new business model) both involves the marketing function and requires some degree of experimentation. Apart from R&D in an engineering-focused business, no area of the firm better lends itself to experimentation than marketing. The students devised a range of experiments to test market segmentation, brand strategies and messaging, and marketing channels. They deployed experiments throughout the development process, beginning during the eight-week course and continuing as a smaller cadre of especially involved students for several months after the course concluded.[4]

In one of its earliest experiments, the entire class tested the product's salability by consulting a tried-and-true research sample: families and friends. Over the Thanksgiving break, the students fanned out with a goal to see how many TerraPasses they could sell. Beyond how many, they wanted to learn three key things that would help shape the future sales and marketing strategy:

- How diverse was the potential individual market? The team predicted that it might be limited to the segment of green consumers, but that was purely a guess.

- What sort of sales pitch worked best? Would prospects have the patience for an explanation of how carbon exchanges operated? Or was simpler better, with the focus kept mainly on the social good of facilitated carbon reductions?

- How would prospects react to the pricing model?

The students sold nearly two hundred TerraPasses. Within the demographic of reasonably affluent middle-class consumers (comprising family and friends), buyers willing to pay a relatively small sum to help the environment proved to be somewhat more diverse than the predicted green segment. For example, although roughly 8 percent of customers were self-identified, environmentally aware owners of hybrid cars, a slightly larger 8.9 percent owned large SUVs. This helped the team refine a market-segmentation model that measured two variables: the extent to which individuals were personally concerned about the environment and the extent to which they believed that business could be a positive force in solving environmental problems. The sweet spot for Terra-Pass appeared to be among pro-business environmentalists, people who tended to be highly educated and quite affluent.

The Thanksgiving sales experiment also yielded some important clues to future promotional tactics. For example, without much prompting, buyers responded favorably to the novelty of the Terrapass idea—that drivers could use the service in order to easily and efficiently "pay for their sins." However, they were less receptive to the somewhat complicated information about the workings of carbon exchanges. This led the brand management and public relations teams to focus less on the underlying mechanisms of offsets and exchanges and more on the ease-of-use and social-good aspects. In marketing, simple messages are best, as shown by the clever TerraPass bumper-sticker copy: "Clean Up After Your Car."

Very few buyers had any objection to the price points. Feedback was especially positive about the way the three tiers sensibly related pricing to a vehicle's fuel efficiency. However, owners of hybrids proposed adding a lower-priced tier for ultra-fuel-efficient vehicles, an idea that was later implemented. In addition, several buyers suggested a possible TerraPass brand extension into air travel, also a significant source of greenhouse gases. In all, more than 80 percent of the first two hundred TerraPass customers reported that they had told others about the business.

The TerraPass model relied on a website as its primary sales channel. Among other things, email marketing pitches could efficiently drive traffic back to the site, providing an easy way of measuring response to particular marketing messages and of capturing additional customer information (age, income, educational level, profession). Zip codes alone were a trove of reliable demographic data. As volume to the website grew over the weeks, a picture of the customer segment became clearer. By the time the course ended in December, the students knew that most of the early buyers were clustered in semi-urban areas and university towns, particularly in blue states like Vermont, and that virtually all of them came from high-income counties. Over time, a consistent 5 percent of visitors to the TerraPass website became members.

The spring-semester Skunk Works group focused almost entirely on finding the best way of reaching the Terrapass sweet spot of pro-business environmentalists. To that end, it conducted an assortment of quick, relatively inexpensive marketing experiments:[5]

- **Marketing alliances.** The team negotiated partnerships with Ford Motor Co. and with the travel website Expedia to offer carbon reductions linked to purchases of new cars and airline tickets. In addition, TerraPass offered to offset, at its own expense, the carbon production of Xootr LLC, a small manufacturer of bikes and scooters. In exchange, Xootr wrote about TerraPass's role in implementing the offset in an email newsletter sent to seven thousand customers. Together, these initiatives produced only modest results.

- **Direct mail (postal).** At the recommendation of a wind-energy marketer, the team sent two thousand postcards (at a cost of $1,400) to addresses in a Palo Alto, California, zip code, referring recipients to a special tracking URL; this led to twenty-three online sessions and three sales.

- **Direct mail (email).** Through an email list provider, the team sent a clickable message to fourteen thousand people (at a cost of $900) who had expressed interest in environmental issues. Of the recipients, 669 clicked back to the TerraPass website, leading to only four sales.

- **Flyers.** The students stuck 750 glossy color postcard-size flyers on car windshields at a farmers' market near Philadelphia and in a nearby park. Though it was hard to precisely track results, by cross-referencing zip codes, the team concluded that the effort produced four sales.

- **Event marketing.** The team had booths at two environmentally themed outdoor events—one in Arizona (at a cost of $2,500) and one in the Philadelphia area (free, except for staff time). It was a good way of building awareness among natural prospects. Still, the Philadelphia event led to only three sales and the Arizona event led to eight.

- **Web marketing.** Two team members devoted most of their time to web marketing. They joined forums and posted on influential, environmentally focused websites. They sent information to the editors and owners of sites whose audiences likely overlapped the TerraPass segment. Over time, they saw that much of the traffic to the TerraPass website originated from a few main sources: a forum for Prius owners; the website of environmental advocate David Suzuki; and the website of the syndicated NPR automotive show, *Car Talk*.

However, the greatest marketing value by far came from favorable press coverage, the earliest examples of which occurred before the course concluded in December. The team learned that when it pitched TerraPass as an automotive story, the resulting articles led to fewer sales than when they focused on the business model's "cool factor." Early on, there were articles in the *L.A. Times* and the *Philadelphia Inquirer*. These in turn got picked up by other media outlets.

The Skunk Works group had two people working primarily on public relations. It also hired a public relations consultant, who sent material about TerraPass to the PR firm's database of fourteen thousand journalists and also worked on a publicity stunt to pressure California Governor Arnold Schwarzenegger to buy TerraPasses for each of his eleven Hummers. Together, these efforts led to a full-page article in *Wired* magazine that drove eight hundred website visitors; Yahoo! featured TerraPass as a "Daily Pick" on its home page (twelve thousand clicks); and CNN.com gave it a spot on its home page. TerraPass ultimately wound up on a 2005 *New York Times* list of top-fifty innovative ideas.

TerraPass Postmortem

As a simple test of the proposition that an inexperienced team can quickly conceive, develop, and execute a promising business model innovation, the student-staffed TerraPass launch was a convincing success. When the six weeks were up, the class had spent less than its $5,000 budget and, after expenses, brought in revenues of roughly $8,000 from the three hundred or so TerraPasses sold to that point. Although we had hopes that the class might produce a start-up business with a shot at longevity, our main purposes were academic—to teach MBA students about the potential of business model innovation (and, of course, to help Karl Ulrich ease his conscience).

On balance, the students performed admirably. As you might expect, a small number of them were more eager and active contributors to the project than others.[6] But we became even more convinced of the Archimedean power of BMI. Moreover, we have no doubt that a small group of smart, experienced businesspeople would have been able to accomplish even more, and in less time, than did our class of forty-one MBA candidates.

Still, the TerraPass experience surpassed our expectations. In early 2005, there were approximately twenty-four hundred subscribers. By the start of the 2005 academic year, we applied for and eventually received a $50,000 grant from the Rockefeller Foundation to pay the salary of founding CEO Tom Arnold. Arnold, who graduated from Wharton in the spring of 2005, wanted to develop the business further. He moved the business to San Francisco and set up shop with a handful of employees. By June 2007, TerraPass had received $5.8 million in venture funding and was bringing in annual revenues of more than $3 million.

In succeeding years, after the growth of its early post-launch period tapered off, the business shifted its emphasis in various ways. Among its strongest recent offerings, for example, is a service that consults to businesses on how to take responsibility for their carbon footprints, both by making their operational practices greener and by participating in offset markets. This is, of course, further evidence that your business models need ongoing attention. Every implementation begins an indeterminate cycle. Like fruit trees, business models need to be regularly tended, trimmed, and nourished in order to perform at their peak.

The TerraPass case is not exactly typical. But as you go forward with your own BMI initiatives, we suspect you will find that *none* are typical. That is because of the great variability within industries and organizations: different people with different strengths coping with unique competitive realities in distinct cultures governed by a complex stew of processes, policies, and management philosophies. Thus, we believe that the most useful aspect of our framework is its applicability to almost any set of circumstances, no matter how different it may be from all others. The more BMI experience you acquire, the likelier it is that you will value the framework's broad utility, gaining confidence that you can make it work for whatever challenges your business encounters.

CHAPTER 8

The Next Business Revolution?

We feel the stirrings of a revolution in business model innovation. After all the years we've spent working in this
field, we believe that the lessons of BMI's potential are
finally breaking through. To be sure, there have always
been creative people more interested in changing the way
value is created or work gets done than in building a better mousetrap. Lately, however, we have seen the focus
on BMI becoming ever more intense in many different
arenas.

Some of that intensity is fueled by the type of frustration that people often experience when they interact with
government bureaucracies. Inspired to break that cycle
of frustration, a nonprofit organization called Code for
America (CFA) brings together software programmers,

local governments, and citizens in a collaborative effort to identify long-standing government inefficiencies and develop web applications to overcome them.

The CFA ethos is to code fast, cheap, clot-busting solutions that change the way city governments work. One CFA project, highlighted recently in a National Public Radio report from Kansas City, showed how the group's coders brainstormed and created an application that streamlined the process of securing the rights to develop abandoned properties.[1] The app—designed during an overnight coding session based on input from citizens and a local economic-development group—automatically and seamlessly vacuums up data from multiple agencies in a matter of minutes. Without such a tool, anyone seeking to develop a property would have to spend weeks or longer trying to penetrate the bureaucracy of several agencies.

In essence, CFA changes the business models of the governments it works with from the outside in, using software to make sense of bureaucratic mysteries without needing to make the mysteries disappear. In the example, CFA didn't reorganize the agencies in any fundamental sense; rather it made captive data more useful and more easily accessible to citizens who need it.

There is more to the CFA value proposition than the sum of the apps it creates. Because of the inclusive, collaborative process it follows in all of its engagements, it leaves cities better off by creating new links between governments, local businesses, citizens, and private social-services groups. In reality, CFA's ultimate mission is to facilitate a more active, accountable, and empowered model of citizenship. As founder Jennifer Pahlka put it in a 2012 TED talk, citizens "have to engage with the machinery of government . . . We're not going to fix government until we fix citizenship."[2]

We have seen a similar mission of determined reinvention in some of the businesses we have worked with. Motivated by the belief that their firms need to become more continuously adaptive, growing numbers of client company CEOs are making a commitment to embed business model innovation in their organizations—to make it part of the everyday thought process.

Too often, managers tend to see innovation as someone else's job—a black box owned by clever geeks and engineers. But business model innovation is different. As we have said, any reasonably experienced manager can learn to build new value out of business models. Just as CFA wants to create a new model for citizenship, businesses increasingly need to spread the BMI mind-set—and permission to apply it—more broadly. They need to change the way they change by fostering cultures that are more receptive to reinvention as a continuous process, not just an event.

Business model innovation is well suited to this more democratized view of innovation. Within many organizations, the population of those who are knowledgeable about and accountable for BMI projects is beginning to expand. Take, for example, our open-ended work with Sberbank, Russia's largest and Europe's third-largest bank. Every year, starting in 2011, we have worked with a new group of five hundred Sberbank managers to coach them on how to conceive and execute BMI projects. In a company of more than 250,000 employees, working at such a scale is imperative. Our goal with each group of managers is to propagate the BMI method throughout the bank in order to help Sberbank transform itself from a lumbering, Soviet-style behemoth into a modern banking enterprise. Over the past couple of years, we have helped managers develop projects large and small, with ambitions ranging from modest operational changes to those with significant strategic implications.

ATMs alone accounted for both types of changes. On the operational side was a project to dramatically reduce the amount of cash stored in the bank's thousands of ATMs, many of which held far more value than usage patterns suggested was needed. Since the excess cash held in ATMs is unavailable for other uses, the bank was needlessly sacrificing potentially valuable liquidity. More strategic was a proposal to create a new revenue stream by allowing Sberbank's ATM service department to maintain not only its own machines but also those of other banks, for which Sberbank could provide service more efficiently and economically than other organizations could manage internally.

Although not all of our participants' ideas were implemented, the process of generating and refining them nonetheless had a profound effect on the way bank managers thought about innovation. As one of the stars of our previous year's program remarked when addressing this year's participants, "[T]his approach will transform you forever. It will change all stereotypes, awaken the brain, enthuse creativity, and help you understand the world. But you need to be ready for these dramatic changes."[3] Naturally, the benefits of a program like this aren't limited to the managers we work with directly; each of them influences others. In this way, understanding spreads, both laterally and at least one further layer down.

Due in large part to adopting a consistent, wide-scale approach to innovation, Sberbank has moved rapidly from its old roots toward its vision of becoming one of the best financial services companies in the world. Not surprisingly, there were numerous inefficiencies—related to both information and incentive-alignment risks—that were relics from the old Soviet era. Eliminating these inefficiencies led quickly to superior performance. In 2012, *The Economist* named Sberbank the second-best-performing stock, worldwide, over the past ten years—a small increment behind only Apple and ahead of such stellar companies as Amazon.[4]

Naturally, such dramatic changes have many ingredients. Chief among them at Sberbank was the commitment from top leadership that the bank's transformation was an urgent priority, and that legacy practices would not be allowed to get in the way. (After all, in a large, established organization like Sberbank, every legacy decision has a loyal constituency that has to be persuaded to change.) It was also important that the bank had an abundance of well-defined inefficiencies on which managers could focus. In addition, leaders and managers alike understood that intrapreneurial change is difficult and must be given priority among other day-to-day activities. At Sberbank, this idea became part of an ongoing program of education to which the CEO German Gref lent his direct and visible support, personally opening the program and, at its conclusion, giving the participants their certificates of completion. Finally, it was an accepted fact that every innovation would require patient experimentation, with the results collected, analyzed, and incorporated in new iterations.

We have learned from the Sberbank experience that business model innovation must be framed as a continuing program of organizational rejuvenation. Increasingly, modern organizations will survive *only* through reinvention. For that reason, we have also been greatly encouraged and inspired to see how a leading firm in an industry as natively conservative as banking could embrace an activity that is so disruptive of the status quo. Sberbank has done vastly more than simply experiment with BMI; it has made it a significant new discipline and placed it at the center of its transformation strategy.

We see other exciting trends as well. The boundaries between an institution and its outside constituents are increasingly blurred. Through social media and other means, outsiders can exert extraordinary pressure on many different kinds of organizations. As in the case of Code for America, this pressure is sometimes organized and programmatic (no pun intended), and may be welcomed—or even instigated—by the institution itself. In other cases, it can be as spontaneous as a brush fire when an organization makes a wrong move.

Whether welcome or unsought, this kind of pressure often presents an opportunity to improve the way you do business. In the best of cases, firms have adapted their business models to more easily incorporate outside thinking—in the form of open innovation or crowdsourcing—in order to tap the surprising value it can offer (Kickstarter, MyFab, InnoCentive, and many others). Firms that are able to transition from resenting the interference of outsiders to explicitly inviting their participation stand to harness an important force multiplier and, potentially, a hedge against disruptive change. After all of the embarrassments businesses have suffered in highly public social-media put-downs, the message is finally getting through that those who fail to take the initiative will sooner or later find themselves backed into a corner.

We are likewise encouraged to see that more organizations are creating an official innovation leadership role, often with the title of chief innovation officer (or CINO, to avoid confusion with the chief information officer). While it's true that such roles can be a way for the CEO to designate an official scapegoat, they also signal to the organization that the activities subsumed in the jobholder's responsibilities are vitally important to the firm. Naturally, we hope that those who hold the title will include BMI initiatives in their purview. Since the most widely accepted definitions of the role emphasize the CINO's responsibility to develop new lines of business to drive future growth, business models should be a key focus of his or her work.

It will be interesting to see how the CINO role plays out. The most promising development might be a leadership approach that can recognize the distinctly different kinds of value offered by BMI and traditional R&D as well as understand how BMI can be used to help tangible, R&D products get traction in the market, as we saw in the example of Netafim in chapter 5. The ability to effectively orchestrate different modes of innovation to achieve complementary benefits will be a hallmark of excellent innovation governance.

Perhaps the greatest source of our optimism about the BMI field is the fact that business leaders, for the past two decades, have had many opportunities to see how a truly well-conceived and executed business model provides a decisive competitive advantage. Optimized business models drive down risk and deliver measurably better performance. That is the opportunity we hope our book helps you pursue. If a slow-moving institution like an old-school Soviet bank can escape the shackles of the past to surpass some of the world's best financial performers, imagine what your own enterprise might be able to accomplish.

We hope that our framework and examples have given you the concepts and tools with which to innovate successful new business models. As you can now appreciate, BMI opportunities often hide in plain sight. They lie buried within companies' business models, becoming obvious only when a competitor seizes the day and begins outperforming the rest of the pack. This is what happened with Dell and Zara, both largely unknown until they shook up their slumbering industries.

It is easy to look at an innovative business model and recognize that it has vastly improved on the status quo. But it's another thing entirely to reverse-engineer the new business model, show what distinguishes it from what it replaced, and explain how it changed the risk equation in order to achieve transforming value. That's what we've done in this book. We have extrapolated general principles that you can apply to produce reliable, repeatable innovations to achieve transformative benefits in a wide range of industries and circumstances.

We are naturally eager for you to let us know how you fare in applying our framework and turning old business models into new ones. Visit us at defineyourcompany.com. Write to us. Call. But beyond all: innovate!

NOTES

Chapter 1

1. Most of the book's references to risk address one or both of these two varieties. However, we will occasionally refer as well to financial, technological, or other kinds of risk. In general, we believe that by mitigating information and incentive-alignment risks, you can often improve your firm's ability to tolerate these other risk categories.

2. Andrew Martin, "Car Sharing Catches On as Zipcar Sells to Avis," *New York Times*, January 2, 2013.

3. Sumner Redstone, *A Passion to Win* (New York: Simon & Schuster, 2001), 284.

4. J. H. Mortimer, "Vertical Contracts in the Video Rental Industry," *Review of Economic Studies* 75 (2008): 165–199. Mortimer attributes a 20 percent boost in industry profits solely to revenue-sharing contracts.

5. Vijay Govindarajan and Chris Trimble, "The CEO's Role in Business Model Reinvention," *Harvard Business Review*, January–February 2011, 108–114.

Chapter 2

1. Marshall Goldsmith, *What Got You Here Won't Get You There* (New York: Hyperion, 2007).

2. An argument can be made that public companies should create shareholder value. However, shareholder value is difficult for any manager to influence; in any case, managers of a company are legally obligated to maximize only profits, not shareholder wealth. So, we will stick with profits in this book.

3. See, for instance, Mark W. Johnson, Clayton M. Christensen, and Henning Kagermann, "Reinventing Your Business Model," *Harvard Business Review*, December 2008, 50–59.

4. Michael Dell and Catherine Fredman, *Direct from Dell* (New York: HarperBusiness, 1999), 22.

5. "Nintendo Plays It a Wii Bit Cautious," *Wall Street Journal*, December 7, 2007.

6. "A Year Later, the Same Scene: Long Lines for the Elusive Wii," *New York Times*, December 14, 2007.

7. See http://en.wikipedia.org/wiki/5_Whys.

8. Nicolas Harle, Michael Pich, and Ludo Van der Heyden, "Marks & Spencer and Zara: Process Competition in the Textile Apparel Industry," Case 02/2002-4974 (Fontainebleau, France: INSEAD, 2002).

Chapter 3

1. Bryant Urstadt, "What Amazon Fears Most: Diapers," *Bloomberg Businessweek*, October 7, 2010, http://www.businessweek.com/magazine/content/10_42/b4199062749187.htm#p2.

2. Ibid.

3. "The Gruesome Math of Hospital Infections," *CNN.com*, April 14, 2011, http://thechart.blogs.cnn.com/2011/04/14/the-gruesome-math-of-hospital-infections/.

4. CVS Caremark Corporation, 2011 Annual Report.

5. James Heskett, "Shouldice Hospital Limited," Case 9-683-068 (Boston: Harvard Business School, 2003).

6. "And the Winners Were . . . ," *The Economist*, December 3, 2011, http://www.economist.com/node/21540389.

7. Geeta Anand, "The Henry Ford of Heart Surgery," *Wall Street Journal*, November 25, 2009.

8. Alex Taylor III, "Volkswagen: Das Auto Giant," *Fortune*, July 10, 2012, http://management.fortune.cnn.com/2012/07/10/global-500-volkswagen/.

9. Manu Goyal and Serguei Netessine, "Strategic Technology Choice and Capacity Investment under Demand Uncertainty," *Management Science* 53, no. 2 (2007): 192–207.

10. Ramon Casadesus-Masanell and Jorge Tarziján, "When One Business Model Isn't Enough," *Harvard Business Review*, January–February 2012, 132–137.

11. See http://www.tankersinternational.com/.

12. For information on how the pool works, see http://www .tankersinternational.com/how_the_pool_works.php.

13. For an example of compensation calculation, see "A Closer Look at Commercial Shipping Pools," *OSG Signal*, Winter 2009, http:// www.osg.com/index.cfm?pageid=74&itemid=13.

14. See http://en.wikipedia.org/wiki/Electronics_manufacturing _services.

15. See http://en.wikipedia.org/wiki/Correlation_and_dependence.

Chapter 4

1. Edward Feitzinger and Hau L. Lee, "Mass Customization at Hewlett-Packard: The Power of Postponement," *Harvard Business Review*, January–February 1997, 116–121.

2. Stephanie Clifford, "Retail Frenzy: Prices on the Web to Adjust Hourly," *New York Times*, November 30, 2012, http://www.nytimes .com/2012/12/01/business/online-retailers-rush-to-adjust-prices-in -real-time.html; and Stephanie Clifford, "Keeping an Eye on Bouncing Prices Online," *New York Times*, January 27, 2013, http://www.nytimes .com/2013/01/28/business/new-online-price-trackers-alert-shoppers-to -good-deals.html.

3. See Rich Metters, Carrie Crystal, Mark Ferguson, Laura Harrison, John Higbie, Stan Ward, Bruce Barfield, Tammy Farley, Ahmet Kuyumcu, and Amar R. Duggasani, "The 'Killer Application' of Revenue Management: Harrah's Cherokee Casino and Hotel," *Interfaces* 38, no. 3 (2008): 161–175.

4. Hau Lee, Seungjin Whang, Kamram Ahsan, Earl Gordon, Amir Faragalla, Asha Jain, Abid Mohsin, and Shi Guangyu, "Harrah's Entertainment Inc.: Real-Time CRM in a Service Supply Chain," Case GS50-PDF-ENG (Palo Alto, CA: Stanford Graduate School of Business, 2006).

5. For more information on the Ansari X Prize, see http://space .xprize.org/ansari-x-prize.

6. Karim R. Lakhani, "InnoCentive.com (A)," Case 9-608-170 (Boston: Harvard Business School, 2008), and Karan Girotra and Christian Terwiesch, "Hypios, Inc.," Teaching Case (INSEAD-Wharton, 2010).

7. Tournaments place the burden of investment on the individuals or candidates in the contest; these individuals have the best information on their abilities and the technologies' performance. Further, they are often motivated by the allure of enhanced reputation achieved by demonstrating their skills to a group larger than just the solution seeker. This motivates them to make higher investments than the seeker would find it rational to make, thereby creating value for all actors in this ecosystem.

8. For more on LiveOps, see http://www.crunchbase.com/company/liveops.

9. S. Netessine and V. Yakubovich, "The Darwinian Workplace," *Harvard Business Review*, May 2012, 25–28.

10. Although MyFab's experiment with decision splitting was successful, the firm has evolved to a point where it no longer regards voting as essential to its strategy.

11. James Surowiecki, *The Wisdom of Crowds* (New York: Anchor Books, 2005).

12. For statistics on Kickstarter, see http://www.kickstarter.com/help/stats.

13. For more on Kickstarter, see http://en.wikipedia.org/wiki/Kickstarter and http://www.kickstarter.com.

14. S. Marinesi's and K. Girotra's "Use and Design of Customer Voting Systems" (unpublished manuscript, 2012) analyzes these new customer voting systems and identifies guidelines for the design and implementation of such systems in a wide range of industries.

Chapter 5

1. See http://www.vendormanagedinventory.com/.

2. Bala Iyer and Thomas H. Davenport, "Reverse Engineering Google's Innovation Machine," *Harvard Business Review*, April 2008, 58–68.

3. Muse was developed by Objective Logistics Inc., a small Cambridge, Massachusetts, start-up. One of the authors is both an adviser and an investor.

4. Eric von Hippel, Susumu Ogawa, and Jeroen P. J. De Jong, "The Age of the Consumer-Innovator," *MIT Sloan Management Review*, Fall 2011, 27–35.

5. Here and later, see Serguei Netessine, "Online Book Retailing: Operational Strategies," Case (Philadelphia: The Wharton School, 2009).

6. See http://www.dropship.com/.

7. For academic analysis of the connection between drop-shipping and internet retailer bankruptcy, see T. Randall, S. Netessine, and N. Rudi, "An Empirical Examination of the Decision to Invest in Fulfillment Capabilities: A Study of Internet Retailers," *Management Science* 52, no. 4 (2006): 567–580.

8. See http://en.wikipedia.org/wiki/Irrigation.

9. See http://en.wikipedia.org/wiki/Drip_irrigation.

10. Here and later, the source of information is Hau Lee and Guy Michlin "Netafim: Migrating from Products to Solutions," Case GS-46 (Palo Alto, CA: Stanford Graduate School of Business, 2006).

11. "Avoiding Water Wars: Water Scarcity and Central Asia's Growing Importance for Stability in Afghanistan and Pakistan," Majority Staff Report for the Committee on Foreign Relations, US Senate, February 2011.

12. For example, Karina Schoengold and David Zilberman, "Water and Development: The Importance of Irrigation in Developing Countries" (unpublished working paper, 2004).

13. See http://en.wikipedia.org/wiki/Moral_hazard.

14. Ibid.

15. See http://en.wikipedia.org/wiki/Efficient_energy_use.

16. See http://en.wikipedia.org/wiki/Energy_service_company.

17. Elisa Wood, "Energy Efficiency Service Companies Missed the Memo," *RenewableEnergyWorld.com*, June 25, 2010, http://www.renewableenergyworld.com/rea/blog/post/2010/06/energy-efficiency-service-companies-missed-the-memo.

18. See http://en.wikipedia.org/wiki/Jevons_paradox.

19. For more on contract design for ESCO, see Sam Aflaki, "The Effect of Environmental Uncertainty on the Tragedy of the Commons," 2010/84/DS (working paper), http://www.insead.edu/facultyresearch/research/details_papers.cfm?id=28346.

Chapter 6

1. Jose A. Guajardo, Morris A. Cohen, Sang-Hyun Kim, and Serguei Netessine. "Impact of Performance-Based Contracting on Product Reliability: An Empirical Analysis," *Management Science* 58, no. 5 (2012): 961–979.

2. Victor K. Fung, William K. Fung, and Yoram (Jerry) R. Wind, *Competing in a Flat World: Building Enterprises for a Borderless World*, 1st ed. (Upper Saddle River, NJ: Pearson Prentice Hall, 2007).

3. For a formal treatment of this argument, see E. Belavina and K. Girotra, "The Relational Advantages of Intermediation," *Management Science* 58, no. 9 (2012): 1614–1631.

4. For a list of countries by total health expenditure (PPP) per capita, see http://en.wikipedia.org/wiki/List_of_countries_by_total_health_expenditure_%28PPP%29_per_capita.

5. "World Health Organization Assesses the World's Health Systems," World Health Report 2000, http://www.who.int/whr/2000/media_centre/press_release/en/.

6. Here and later, see C. Christensen, J. H. Grossman, and J. Hwang, *The Innovator's Prescription: A Disruptive Solution for Health Care* (New York: McGraw-Hill, 2009), chap. 6.

7. See V. Fuhrmans, "Radical Surgery: One Cure for High Health Costs: In-House Clinics at Companies," *Wall Street Journal*, February 11, 2005.

8. Tiffay O'Callaghan, "Too Many C-Sections: Docs Rethink Induced Labor," *TIME*, August 2, 2010.

9. Paula S. Katz, "Big Employers Bring Health Care In-House," ACP *Observer*, January–February 2007, http://www.acpinternist.org/archives/2007/01/clinics.htm.

10. See S. H. Jain and D. Roble, "Gainsharing in Healthcare: Meeting the Quality-of-Care Challenge," *Healthcare Financial Management* 62, no. 3 (2008): 72–78.

11. CMS, "Medicare Gain-Sharing Demonstration: Report to Congress on Quality Improvement and Savings," Report to Congress, March 28, 2011.

12. For more on bundled payment, see http://en.wikipedia.org/wiki/Bundled_payment.

Chapter 7

1. TerraPass was developed by a class of Wharton MBA students under the direction of Karl Ulrich and Karan Girotra. Girotra, as one of the founders, formerly held a significant stake in the company but is no longer involved.

2. Interested readers can learn more about TerraPass from two cases: a 2008 Wharton School case written by Karl Ulrich ("TerraPass, Inc.," teaching case [Philadelphia: Wharton School, 2008]), and a 2009 Stanford Graduate School of Business case, written by Bethany Coates under the supervision of Chuck Holloway ("TerraPass," Case E-311 [Palo Alto, CA: Stanford Graduate School of Business, 2009]). Both describe key aspects of the TerraPass project and its development as a business.

3. A single unit of carbon offset is defined as a means of reducing carbon dioxide—or some other greenhouse gas—by one metric ton.

4. The basic TerraPass business model debuted at the end of the six-week course. However, a handful of students chose to continue refining it during the spring semester. It was this group—working with Karan Girotra and Karl Ulrich, and under the leadership of MBA student Tom Arnold (who ultimately became the company's first CEO)—that performed most of the marketing experiments, using $50,000 raised from angel investors.

5. In the 2004–2005 time frame of TerraPass's early history, the tools available for identifying and reaching a small niche market were relatively crude compared with what exists today. For that reason, nearly all of the team's experiments were disappointing. PR was the sole bright spot and main source of customers.

6. In addition to grades, the students were awarded shares of stock in TerraPass in proportion to the time they spent working on the project and the quality of their contributions. When TerraPass won its first

round of financing, students were able to sell their shares, an average allotment of which would have yielded roughly $15,000 per person.

Chapter 8

1. Laura Ziegler, "How Code for America Apps Benefit Kansas City," *NPR*, May 18, 2013, http://www.npr.org/2013/05/28/186861864/how-apps-help-kansas-city-work-better.

2. Jennifer Pahlka, "Coding a Better Government," TED Talk, February 2012, http://www.ted.com/talks/jennifer_pahlka_coding_a_better_government.html.

3. From comments of Vasily Mischenko, during the graduation ceremony speech, September 2012, class of 2011–2012.

4. A 2002 investment of $100 in Sberbank stock was worth $3,722 in 2012 (a comparable investment in Apple yielded $3,919). See "Invest in a Time Machine: The Best and Worst Stocks of the Past Decade," *The Economist*, February 18, 2012, http://www.economist.com/node/21547810.

INDEX

Note: Page numbers followed by *f* refer to figures; page numbers followed by *t* refer to tables.

ACKNOWLEDGMENTS

Both of us have been fortunate to be a part of two of the world's greatest educational institutions: the Wharton School at the University of Pennsylvania and INSEAD. This book would not be possible without the generous financial support of both schools and support from the Wharton-INSEAD Alliance. Through its exceptional global reach and vast connections with practice, INSEAD endowed us with the platform to learn from businesses, research their business model innovation journeys, and share our learning at its educational programs and public events.

Our academic careers started at Wharton's operations and information management department, where we were influenced by a number of brilliant colleagues including Krishnan Anand, Gérard Cachon, Eric Clemons, Morris Cohen, Marshall Fisher, Noah Gans, Monique Guignard-Spielberg, Jack Hershey, Shawndra Hill, Kartik Hosanagar, Steven Kimbrough, Paul Kleindorfer, Howard Kunreuther, Sergei Savin, Maurice Schweitzer, Uri Simonsohn, Christian Terwiesch, Anita Tucker, Karl

Ulrich, Senthil Veeraraghavan, and Yu-Sheng Zheng. Our daily interactions with them, inspirational discussions at lunches and seminars, and heated arguments over coffee shaped the early ideas for this book. We want to particularly acknowledge the inspiration we got from Gérard Cachon, Christian Terwiesch, and Karl Ulrich, whose classes, books, and academic papers prompted us to think about innovation in the first place.

We are equally indebted to our INSEAD colleagues, who helped us develop the ideas in this book and bring them to fruition. We are grateful to our colleagues Ben Bensaou, Shantanu Bhattacharya, Steve Chick, Sameer Hasija, Jürgen Mihm, Michael Pich, Dana Popescu, Nils Rudi, Manuel Sosa, Luk Van Wassenhove, Ludo Van der Heyden, Enver Yücesan, and Francis de Véricourt. As we continued our innovation journey, all of them helped us with formalizing our theory by providing a sounding board, sharing teaching opportunities, and collaborating on a variety of projects. We want to especially acknowledge the input of Ludo Van der Heyden, whose work on business model innovation nudged us in the right direction and whose creative teaching of this subject led us to start this project.

Both of us have been fortunate to work with numerous doctoral students at Wharton and INSEAD, and their hard work is behind many academic papers that support ideas in this book. Most of these students are now prominent academics or distinguished practitioners, and we can only hope that this book will influence them in the same way they influenced us. Our gratitude goes to (in chronological order) Fuqiang Zhang (Washington University, St. Louis), Wenqiang Xiao (NYU), Manu Goyal (University of Utah), Jayanth Krishnan (McKinsey), Sergey Rumyantsev (Prosiris Capital Management), Sang-Hyun Kim (Yale), Robert Swinney (Duke), Kinshuk Jerath (Columbia University), Jun Li (Michigan), Jose Guajardo (Berkeley), Wenjie Tang (Instituto de Impresa), Tom Tan (Southern Methodist University), Sam Aflaki (HEC), Elena Belavina (Chicago), Buket Avci (Singapore Management University), Nitish Jain (LBS), Simone Marinesi (Wharton), Konstantinos Stouras (still at INSEAD), Ashish Kabra (still at INSEAD), and Christophe Pennetier (still at INSEAD).

Over the years, many of our academic colleagues helped us shape our ideas with discussions, advice, and encouragement, all of which contributed to our writing of this book. We wish to acknowledge Kamalini Ramdas (LBS), Sezer Ulku (Georgetown), Beril Toktay (Georgia Tech), and Stelios Kavadias (Cambridge) for helping test teaching materials related to the book; Frances Frei (Harvard) for her inspirational advice and encouragement; Valery Yakubovich (ESSEC) for research collaborations; Subi Rangan (INSEAD) for helping us tighten our theory; and Laurence Capron (INSEAD) and Ron

Adner (Dartmouth College) for discussing book writing and publication strategy.

Participants in our executive programs played an essential role in shaping this book. Our discussions with program participants helped us refine our theory, and their continuing engagement after our programs provided us with many examples validating our theories. Their careful reading of chapters from the book and their subsequent critiques helped us better articulate our ideas. At the end of each program, we made a call for focus on business model innovation, and hundreds of our program participants answered this call. While there are too many to list here, we are forever grateful to our program participants for sharing their innovation journeys with us and letting us learn from them.

Examples and ideas in this book have also been shaped by our collaboration with practicing executives. Some went far and beyond, helping us understand their organizations, and their companies occupy a prominent space in the book as a result of these collaborations. We are grateful to (in no particular order) Marc Lore (cofounder and CEO at Quidsi), Scott Hilton (vice president of operations at Quidsi), Matthew Grace (cofounder and chief technology officer at Objective Logistics), Philip Beauregard (cofounder and CEO at Objective Logistics), Jesus Eschevarria (chief communications officer at Inditex), Tom

Arnold (CEO at TerraPass), Mark Pringle (vice president of worldwide procurement at Dell), Kevin Brown (chief supply chain officer at Dell), Hermann Simon (chairman at Simon-Kucher & Partners), Gang Yu (former vice president of global supply chain at Amazon.com, former vice president of worldwide procurement at Dell, and chairman of The Store Corporation), and German Gref (president of Sberbank).

Likewise, examples and teachings from this book have been tested by thousands of MBA and EMBA program participants at Wharton and INSEAD. Their critical but fair comments sharpened our theory, and their zealous desire to succeed as entrepreneurs showed again and again that our theory can lead to the creation and growth of new companies. Their energy is the main fuel that inspired this book.

We thank Lew McCreary for exceptional editorial work on the book and David Champion (Harvard Business Review Press) for guiding us from the initial publication of our first *Harvard Business Review* article on the subject all the way to publication of this book.

And, of course, we could not have finished this book without our families; without them, our efforts would not even be worthwhile. Serguei dedicates this book to his wife, Irina, and children, Victoria and Nicholas, and Karan to his parents, Satinder and Jyotsina.

ABOUT THE AUTHORS

KARAN GIROTRA is Professor of Technology and Operations Management at INSEAD, where he teaches and researches entrepreneurship, business model audit, design, and innovation.

Girotra has designed and led workshops on the generation, selection, and refinement of new business opportunities for participants ranging from aspiring entrepreneurs to large corporations around the world, including ABB (US, EMEA, and Asia), Johnson & Johnson (EMEA), International Flavors & Fragrances (US), Orascom Telecom (Lebanon), Bayer (Germany), Sonepar (France), and Yapi Kredi (Turkey). He is a winner of the best professor award in the MBA program at INSEAD, two-time runner-up for the best professor award in the executive MBA program, and four-time winner of the dean's award for excellence in teaching.

In addition to his academic work, Girotra was a founder of TerraPass, Inc., which the *New York Times* identified as one of the most noteworthy ideas of 2005. He continues to actively engage with start-ups as an adviser, investor, and mentor. Some recent start-ups that he's advising are poised to disrupt traditional business models in the residential services, beauty, and automated retail industries.

Girotra holds a PhD in managerial sciences and applied economics from the Wharton School, University of Pennsylvania, an AM degree from the Wharton School, and a Bachelor of Technology degree from the Indian Institute of Technology, Delhi.

Girotra blogs about business model innovation at renaissanceinnovator.com and is a regular contributor to the *Harvard Business Review* blog network. Follow him on Twitter at @GirotraK.

SERGUEI NETESSINE is the Timken Chaired Professor of Global Technology and Innovation at INSEAD and the Research Director of the Wharton-INSEAD Alliance. Prior to joining INSEAD in 2010, he was a faculty member at the Wharton School, University of Pennsylvania, which he joined in 2001.

Originally a computer scientist, Netessine worked for Motorola and Lucent Technologies and then received MS and PhD degrees in operations management from the University of Rochester. His current research focuses on business model innovation and operational excellence; he has worked on these topics with numerous organizations in the United States, Europe, and Asia, including the US Federal Aviation Administration, Lockheed Martin,

Procter & Gamble, McDonald's, Rolls-Royce, Comcast, Expedia, ABB, and the US Air Force. Additionally, he serves on advisory boards of multiple start-up companies. Netessine is a frequent speaker on innovation at industry events, including the World Knowledge Forum.

Netessine has been the recipient of several awards for teaching MBA and executive MBA students at the Wharton School and INSEAD. He frequently teaches in executive education programs. A prolific writer, Netessine has coauthored dozens of academic and management articles, and holds senior editorial positions at several leading academic journals. His work has received extensive media coverage in *CIO Magazine*, the *Economist*, *Forbes*, *Multichannel Merchant*, the *New York Times*, *U.S. News & World Report*, *Strategy & Business*, and others.

Netessine blogs about business model innovation at renaissanceinnovator.com and is a regular contributor to the *Harvard Business Review* blog network. Follow him on Twitter at @snetesin.